ELIJAH,
A MAN OF LIKE NATURE

*(Messages given over the international network
of Back to the Bible Broadcast)*

BY THEODORE H. EPP

*Founder and Director
of Back to the Bible Broadcast*

Back to the Bible
Lincoln, Nebraska 68501

35,000 printed to date—1975
(5-4790—2M—105)
ISBN 0-8474-1297-0

Printed in the United States of America

Foreword

When the enemy of God brought Baal into Israel like a flood, the Spirit of God raised up Elijah against him. The Lord needed a man to stand in the gap and the lowly Tishbite was the man He found. Yet Elijah was as human as the rest of us. Where he differed from the average believer was in his single-minded devotion to God. When God commanded, Elijah obeyed. He was a man of faith whose works of faith will live on.

The spiritual impact of these messages which were first heard on the daily broadcast is cause for rejoicing. We trust that in this printed form they will prove to be of special help in many hearts and homes in the days and months to come, should our Lord tarry.

—John I. Paton
Literature Editor

CONTENTS

CONTENTS

THE MAN ELIJAH

He was a remarkable man, so remarkable in fact, that many Christians are inclined to look upon him as a kind of superhuman being. He lived a busy and useful life, and after his ministry was ended God took him to heaven without dying. Nearly a thousand years later, this man came back to earth and visited the Lord Jesus Christ on a mountain. According to prophecy, this same man will come back and minister on earth for a short time just prior to the Second Coming of Christ. His name is Elijah, a man whom we are inclined to set apart from ordinary servants of the Lord.

Such an estimate, however, is wrong. In the Book of James, we read, "Elias was a man subject to like passions as we are" (5:17). He was after all, a human being like the rest of us. He had emotions and problems, he saw the same ups and downs in his life that all of us face. The Amplified says, "Elijah was a human being with a nature such as we have."

When we compare Elijah's life with David's we find that David had many faults, yet he was called a man after God's own heart. Elijah, on the other hand, has very little recorded against him by way of weaknesses or sins, but we are told that he was a man of "like nature."

To harmonize such evaluations one must know and understand God's viewpoint on things. He knows our frailties and inabilities. We are but weak human flesh, something we must recognize if we would keep our proper perspective on life. We must know that in ourselves we are nothing and that any success we have in our spiritual life and ministry is due to God. David or Elijah left to themselves would have been complete failures, just as we would be. Both men became great because they trusted God. They committed themselves totally to do His will.

In our study of the life of David,* many Christians wrote telling us that they were encouraged to realize how a man with faults and sins was still used of God. David, of course, knew how to deal with his faults in the light of God's truth and how to trust God for great things. Very little is given with regard to Elijah's personal life, but a close study of his life reveals him as a human being like the rest of us. He was a man of like passions or nature. The word "passion" in this context does not mean he was a man with evil habits in the sense of gross sins, but a man with feelings that we would expect in a human being. He was like us in that there were times when he was afraid, and because of his fear he fled. He saw discouragement almost to the point of death. He had the same needs and appetites the rest of us have; and he needed the support that only God can give. He was capable of suffering the same things we suffer, for, after all, he was only a man.

He was subject to the same frailties we are. He had the same nature, the same general kind of disposition all of us are heir to. But because he was taken from this world without dying, some of us hesitate to look on him as a pattern whereby we might be guided in our own spiritual lives.

From both David and Elijah we must learn to look not at the merits and abilities of a man but upon the grace of God. In studying the lives of these great men, we are not unduly exalting them, rather we are exalting the greatness of God.

God has His own measure of greatness, and both David and Elijah fit into that measure. Elijah was a righteous man. He was a man who prayed, a man who believed, and a man who received answers from God. He had some outstanding answers to prayer, for he was a man who dared to believe what God told him.

His prayers of faith are outstanding, yet they do not illustrate the power of the prophet but the power of God in

*Now in the book form, *A Man After the Heart of God,* Back to the Bible Broadcast, $1.50 per copy.

the heart of a man who was humble enough to believe Him.

Elijah's Name

Elijah's name by interpretation means, "My God is power, or Jehovah is my strength." There is a vast difference between the two ideas that the Lord strengthens me and that the Lord is my strength. Paul emphasizes this latter fact in Ephesians 6:10: "Finally, my brethren, be strong in the Lord, and in the power of his might." The apostle does not say that we should ask God for power to overcome this or to give strength for that, but simply trust God to be the Strength and Power needed.

The Apostle Paul is perhaps the greatest exponent of this truth. Christ is made unto us whatever our need is. If it is strength, He is our Strength. If it is holiness, he is made unto us Holiness. If it is righteousness, He is our Righteousness. If it is life, He is our Life. He is what we need, and He is what we need to be.

Think of it this way. There is a difference between God holding a shield before me and the fact that God is my Shield. If God holds a shield before me that shield will provide good protection. But if I realize that He himself is my shield, I not only have protection, but I will be more than conqueror, for He is the Divine Victor.

One day I was reading Ephesians 1:13,14 where it says we are sealed with the Holy Spirit. I read it, "We are sealed BY the Holy Spirit." A dear man of God corrected me by saying, "Brother, it does not say 'by,' it says 'with.'" This makes all the difference in the world. To be sealed by the Holy Spirit simply means that the Holy Spirit is the One who seals us. But if we speak of being sealed with the Holy Spirit, then He is both the Instrument and the Seal.

So it is essential that we recognize Elijah's name means "God is our Strength and Power." It is more than God giving us peace; He is our Peace. It is not only that God gives us strength to do something; but when we realize that God is our Strength, then our resources are as limitless as God himself.

Moses first surrendered himself to God at the age of 40 years. He was willing to become God's man to free the nation of Israel and take them out of the land of Egypt. He believed

God and trusted Him for strength. Then he went out in the strength he trusted God for, but he accomplished very little. He slew one Egyptian and had to flee for his life. At the age of 80, after he had learned to know God in a much more personal way, he returned to Egypt. He did not ask God for strength, instead he returned in the strength of God. He let God undertake for him and recognized that he was merely an instrument in God's hand. The result was that Israel was emancipated and the Egyptian army destroyed. It is not a matter of great faith, but faith in a great God.

Elijah's Background

Elijah is first introduced to us as the Tishbite in the 17th chapter of I Kings. It simply tells us that he was an inhabitant of Gilead. We know very little about him from this standpoint. He came from the mountains of Gilead on the other side of Jordan, from a group that was something of an outcast group. He might have been from the tribe of Manasseh, for that area had been given over to Manasseh's descendants. They were a hill people, strong and rugged, dwelling in rude villages and hardened by life in the open air. The record indicates that Elijah was a powerful man physically, a person strong of mind and earnest in spirit.

His birthplace was the little town of Tishbeh, a small obscure village in the mountains. His formal education was apparently not extensive, and of his early religious training we know next to nothing. He and his fellow Israelites were surrounded by enemies who were idol worshippers; but of Elijah we read, "I have been very jealous for the Lord God of hosts" (I Kings 19:10). We gather from this that he was a man who was separated to God and desirous of seeing God exalted. He must have had a thorough knowledge of the then existing Scriptures among them being the five books of Moses, Joshua, and the Psalms of David.

In his youth he must have pondered at length over the blight of sin that had degraded his people. Then, in his mature manhood, he saw how Jezebel, an ungodly woman from heathen Zidon, brought Baal worship into Israel. This was one of the darkest hours of Israel's history. Jezebel killed all the prophets of God she could put her hands on. Others had to flee for their lives. At one time Elijah thought he was the only one left until God told him that there were 7000 others who had not bowed their knees to Baal. They, however, were in hiding, they were not out working in the open for the Lord. Leading in idol worship were some 850 priests of Baal and the groves whose wages were paid by the state. This was the condition in Israel when Elijah's ministry began.

Elijah's Prayers

Elijah, as we have said, knew the Word of God, and he began to pray in the light of God's promises. He knew for example what Moses had stated in Deuteronomy 11:13-17: "And it shall come to pass, if ye shall hearken diligently unto my commandments which I command you this day, to love the Lord your God, and to serve him with all your heart and with all your soul, That I will give you the rain of your land in his due season, the first rain and the latter rain, that thou mayest gather in thy corn, and thy wine, and thine oil. And I will send grass in thy fields for thy cattle, that thou mayest eat and be full. Take heed to yourselves, that your heart be not deceived, and ye turn aside, and serve other gods, and worship them; And then the Lord's wrath be kindled against you, and he shut up the heaven, that there be no rain, and that the land yield not her fruit; and lest ye perish quickly from off the good land which the Lord giveth you."

Knowing the conditions God said would prevail if the Israelites practiced obedience and knowing what He had promised as judgment if they were disobedient, Elijah prayed that it would not rain. And it did not rain for a period of three and a half years. He prayed again that it should rain and it did. These are good examples of the prayer of faith, for true prayer is laying hold of what God has said in His Word and pleading with Him to do as He has promised.

This is not the only time in the Bible where we find men of God going to the Word to find what God has said and then to pray that God's Word will be fully carried out. True praying is simply taking God at His Word and praying about it. This was how Daniel prayed: "In the first year of Darius the son of Ahasuerus, of the seed of the Medes, which was made king over the realm of the Chaldeans; In the first year of his reign I Daniel understood by books the number of the years, whereof the word of the Lord came to Jeremiah the prophet, that he would accomplish seventy years in the desolations of Jerusalem" (9:1,2).

Daniel read in Jeremiah 25:11,12, that after seventy years captivity, God would forgive His ancient people and bring them back again into their land. On finding this, Daniel set his face to seek the Lord in prayer. It was with fasting and sackcloth and ashes that he prayed to the Lord and made his confession. Daniel expected God to act on the basis of His promise, and God did.

According to the 10th chapter of Daniel, the prophet was "mourning three full weeks." And then he states, "I ate no pleasant bread, neither came flesh nor wine into my mouth, neither did I anoint myself at all, till three whole weeks were fulfilled." All this time he was praying. He was claiming the wonderful promise of God, waiting until assurance from God would come that the promise would be fulfilled.

This was how Elijah prayed also. We are told, "He prayed earnestly." This literally means he prayed in prayer, or as we might say, "He really prayed." His prayers were framed for the ears of God and not for the ears of men. Sometimes people remark, "So and so prays beautifully." Such prayer does not necessarily mean a thing to God. It is prayer directed to the ears of God and not to the ears of men that God hears.

Elijah did not know that there were still 7000 of God's servants remaining in Israel, possibly many of them hiding in the mountains. It was then that Elijah prayed that rain would cease to fall which, of course, meant that drought would come. Some might think this was cruel. It would cause much suffering; even Elijah himself would be affected by it. This made no difference to his thinking, for he based his prayer on God's Word. Since God said this was good for His people if they left Him, then it would be good and not wrong to pray that such chastisement fall upon them. Its purpose was to bring God's people back to Him.

Men need to know that God is the living God. In Elijah's day idols were worshipped, but they were dead things. It was high time that someone demonstrated that God was alive and powerful on behalf of His people. The Israelites needed to know that God's words were not empty utterances and that God would enforce His judgments. In the mystery of God's dealing with men, all He needed was a man to pray. Up to this moment God had withheld judgment, but the time was ripe for God to show His hand.

We read in Psalm 50:21: "These things hast thou done, and I kept silence; thou thoughtest that I was altogether such an one as thyself: but I will reprove thee, and set them in order before thine eyes. Now consider this, ye that forget God, lest I tear you in pieces, and there be none to deliver." Elijah prayed that God might be proven to be God before the eyes of His people.

Would any of us dare to pray for judgment on the nations in the light of the great sins and rebellion against God that we see everywhere? Elijah's prayer had quite an affect upon himself as well as others, but his praying was in the will of God and not on the basis of any personal grudge against others.

Have we asked that the Lord would send an awakening at any cost? Perhaps we have asked God to send an awakening; but have we asked Him to do it at any cost?

I found myself praying just that very way. Realizing something of the conditions of the day, I asked the Lord that there might be an awakening at any cost. But I had to stop and think and consider: Could I honestly say, "at any cost"? Whatever our reactions might be, we can go on to pray, telling the Lord that we are willing to be made willing to include the phrase "at any cost" in our prayers.

A spiritual awakening usually costs. Generally speaking we are too selfish and unconcerned to pray for what will benefit us if it is going to cost suffering or trial, even if the goal will be pleasing to God. So many of us want to live our lives unhindered so that we can go on accumulating money, filling up our bank accounts regardless of what happens to the lost.

Perhaps we have not admitted this to ourselves, but that is the way we are by nature. What needs to take place is for us to become concerned about the Lord's welfare. What crimes against men are to be compared to the high-handed sin that is leveled against God in our day? What are national or personal reverses compared to God's glory and the receiving of His favor?

We are having great prosperity in our country today and are proud of it. But what if we were to face terrible financial reverses? A far greater loss than that, however, would be the loss of God's favor. Much more would be at stake than the loss of material things.

CHAPTER TWO

ELIJAH, GOD'S PROPHET

Elijah had a true sense of values. As a prophet of God he knew what God desired, and he knew that what God desired was best for Israel.

Perhaps we will be inclined to say that we could never pray like Elijah. Remember, God tells us he was a man of "like nature." He was a human being like the rest of us and faced discouragement and dismay. He was as human as anybody could be human. The big difference between Elijah and most of us is that he was all out for God most of the time. A prophet like that had to walk alone for few persons wanted to walk with him.

We read in II Timothy 3:5 of those who have a form of godliness but who deny the power thereof. From such we are to turn away. A true prophet of God will do that. By a prophet, we are not thinking so much of one who foretells but one who tells out God's message. The prophets were not accredited by the religious systems of their day; they did not belong to these systems and did not seem to care that they were not endorsed by them. Very often these prophets were despised and persecuted and hated by religious leaders. The prophets had a special message and a mission to perform in arousing the slumbering conscience of God's people. They were also sent to comfort the people of God, but only an insignificant remnant believed them.

Even though Elijah was obscure in his background, he was called of God to stand before a king. The record is, "And Elijah the Tishbite, who was of the inhabitants of Gilead, said unto Ahab, As the Lord God of Israel liveth, before whom I stand, there shall not be dew nor rain these years, but according to my word" (I Kings 17:1). Elijah could stand before Ahab because he first stood before God. To stand before God we must be cleansed by the blood, reconciled to God through the sacrifice of Jesus Christ. We must be constantly waiting on God, to be committed to Him, ever ready to obey His slightest command. We must be at God's disposal to do little things or big things, whatever it is that God calls upon us to do.

Our concern must be for the Lord and not for ourselves. This was Elijah's attitude, for he was jealous for the Lord God of hosts. This is what the Psalmist tells us in Psalm 37:4: "Delight thyself also in the Lord; and he shall give thee the desires of thine heart." The word "delight" simply means to honor God, to find out what His pleasure is, to do His will and to speak the words that He has given. It is when we delight in Him that we have the right desires and are in a position where God can answer them. God's promise is that if we commit our way to Him, and also trust in Him, He shall bring it to pass.

There are many people today who talk about working for God. But it is not our working for God so much as getting ourselves in line with God so that He can work through us. This involves submission to His will. What I want means nothing; what He wants is everything. Samuel of old cried, "Speak, Lord, for thy servant heareth."

There are times when I have found it necessary to refuse speaking engagements for the simple reason that they will rob me of time with the Lord. A few years ago I was invited by a friend to be with him during New Year's services. Before I was through, I had spoken seven times. I told the good brother that I could never do it again, for it gave me no time for the Lord. We have time for only a fifteen-minute message on our radio broadcasts, but if it is to be of any account, we must prepare by being alone with God for two or three hours at the very least. Remember the Lord Jesus himself sets us the very best example of getting alone with God before ministering to the people.

The Boldness of Elijah

Elijah was a man with a nature like we have. He had a remarkable ministry, but he is not away beyond our reach.

He was a man with special gifts from God and was set apart in a very special way to perform a special ministry. The difference between him and us is due to the special work God had for him and to the fact that he was fully submitted to God. Left to his own resources he became as weak as a child. At one period in his life he was discouraged almost to the point of death. Renewed by God he was as bold as a lion.

He dared to stand before King Ahab and pronounce the judgment of God upon him and his kingdom. The prophet showed no hesitancy here and expected the thing to happen that God said would happen. The basic principle back of this is given us in the New Testament. In Mark 11:22,23 we find the Lord Jesus telling us to "Have faith in God." He continued, "For verily I say unto you, that whosoever shall say unto this mountain, Be thou removed, and be thou cast into the sea; and shall not doubt in his heart, but shall believe that those things which he saith will come to pass; he shall have whatsoever he saith." This is God speaking and it is for us to believe.

The first thing that Elijah did when he stood before Ahab was to remind the king that the God of Israel is a living God. Jezebel had brought Baal worship into Israel and had 850 priests leading in the worship of this dead idol. So the first thing Elijah said was, "As the Lord God of Israel liveth." Like Job before him he could say, "I know that my redeemer liveth." This was in direct contrast to the dead idol of Baal. It was also stated in preparation for what Elijah would prove at a later time on Mount Carmel. That event was still three years in the future, but it was the Living God who acted and demonstrated His power.

How great is our God? It is not so much a question of how great is our faith, but rather how great is our God? That is the important thing. Elijah called on God to witness to His own pronouncements. God had stated that if the Israelites ran after other gods, He would withhold rain from them. Elijah dared to believe God for this and pronounced judgment upon the basis of God's Word. He did not just pray, but he said, "As the Lord God of Israel liveth, before whom I stand, there shall not be dew nor rain these years, but according to my word" (I Kings 17:1). He was able to say this because he knew God and

believed Him. "God is not a man that he should lie; neither the
son of man, that he should repent: hath he said, and shall he
not do it? or hath he spoken, and shall he not make it good?"
(Num. 23:19).

John the Apostle fell prostrate at the feet of Jesus when he
saw Him in a vision on the Isle of Patmos. The record is, "And
when I saw him, I fell at his feet as dead. And he laid his right
hand on me, saying unto me, Fear not; I am the first and the
last: I am he that liveth, and was dead; and, behold, I am alive
for evermore, Amen; and have the keys of hell and of death"
(Rev. 1:17,18). This is our God. This is the God Elijah had. This
is the God of whom he said, "As the Lord God of Israel liveth."

Palestine experienced periods of early and latter rains and
in the interval between, heavy dews at night kept the vegeta-
tion refreshed. But there was nothing that man could do to
cause rain if God withheld the clouds. Man cannot create, that
is the prerogative of God. Science is dabbling around with the
matter of seeding the clouds, but men have to have clouds before they can seed them. This is something that only God can
provide. Man cannot do it.

One day as my wife and I were traveling we heard on the
radio that in our own state of Nebraska some people had hired
an old Indian Chief to see if he could create rain. The thing
that struck us was this, "Are we returning to paganism in our
land?" No wonder God has to speak to us today by means of
storms of hail and rain and floods. Some of them have been
disastrous. God might speak also by withholding rain. Jeremiah raises this question in the 14th chapter of his prophecy,
in verse 22: "Are there any among the vanities of the Gentiles
that can cause rain? or can the heavens give showers? art not
thou he, O Lord our God? therefore we will wait upon thee: for
thou hast made all these things."

We gather from the record that at the time Elijah faced
Ahab with the news of God's judgment, the drought had been
on the land for some six months. This lack of rain was the result of the direct prayer of Elijah who based it on God's state-
ments through Moses in Deuteronomy. The prophet had not
gone to see Ahab immediately but waited until Ahab and the

nation were in dire need of rain. Then he told Ahab that there would be no dew nor rain not only for months but for years— until he, Elijah, gave the word.

Elijah was in a place of danger when he stood before Ahab. The evil woman the king had married sought the life of every servant of God that she could find.

God's prophet had no prestige of position or of wealth that might have made Ahab hesitant about destroying him. Elijah was a rough mountaineer dressed in a garment made from camel's hair, a poor man whose life Ahab might take without any qualms of conscience. Yet the prophet stood before the king and claimed the six-month drought was due to his intercession before God.

How could a man who had no standing socially or governmentally dare to be so bold? The answer lies in I Corinthians: "For ye see your calling, brethren, how that not many wise men after the flesh, not many mighty, not many noble, are called: But God hath chosen the foolish things of the world to confound the wise; and God hath chosen the weak things of the world to confound the things which are mighty; And base things of the world, and things which are despised, hath God chosen, yea, and things which are not, to bring to nought things that are: That no flesh should glory in his presence" (1:26-29).

Elijah was a man of the same nature as we are. He was weak in himself, but he became mighty through God to the place where he could pull down strongholds. This is not something belonging only to Elijah, for these same truths apply to us today. We, too, can be bold in situations when we know we are in the will of God and God is back of us. We may be unknown and have nothing that the world would highly regard such as family, social position or learning; but since it is God who supplies the power, we can accomplish His tasks. We learn from II Corinthians 10 that "though we walk in the flesh, we do not war after the flesh: (For the weapons of our warfare are not carnal, but mighty through God to the pulling down of strong holds;) Casting down imaginations, and every high thing that exalteth itself against the knowledge of God, and bringing into captivity every thought to the obedience of Christ" (vv. 3-5).

The Secret of Elijah's Strength

We, too, can do exploits for God if we will take time as did Elijah to speak before God in the secret place and then go out by faith in the zeal and energy of the Lord to do His work. The first part of his secret was his prayer life.

We must never lose sight of James 5:17: "Elias was a man subject to like passions as we are, and he prayed earnestly that it might not rain: and it rained not on the earth by the space of three years and six months. And he prayed again, and the heaven gave rain, and the earth brought forth her fruit." He was a man of like passions as we are, but he prayed. "He prayed in prayer" is the literal thought here. For at least six months he had been in sincere prayer in the presence of God before he ever entered into the presence of Ahab.

This is the means that God uses with His own people. We learn in Ephesians 6:18 that we are to pray with all supplication in the Spirit. Praying in the Spirit means to be prompted by the Spirit in what we pray for. In Elijah's case, God had decided that the time was ready for the people of Israel to be reminded of what He had told them through Moses. God said that if they would obey, they would be blessed; but if they disobeyed, they would be chastised. God needed a man to ask Him that this judgment be put into effect. He found such a man in Elijah. The prophet gave himself earnestly to prayer and God shut up the heavens so that it did not rain.

When it came time to stand before Ahab, Elijah stood there unafraid because he had knelt in humility before Almighty God. The Lord gives grace to the humble, but He resists the proud. For this reason we are to submit ourselves to God, but we are to resist the Evil One and he will flee from us. "Draw nigh to God, and he will draw nigh to you. Cleanse your hands, ye sinners; and purify your hearts, ye double minded" is the admonition that James gives. Having obeyed this admonition, we can come before God and ask and we will receive. When we are right with God in our hearts, then it is that we ask for the things that please Him and He answers us.

Elijah had a knowledge of God. This was another reason for his strength. He not only knew the names of God and His mighty works, but he had a personal inner knowledge of Him. It was the kind of knowledge of which Paul speaks in Philippians 3:10: "That I may know him, and the power of his resurrection." Ahab did not worship this God but Elijah did. God was a living reality to Elijah. He should be to us also.

There are many persons today who have a very low view of God. They do not understand who He is, or what He wants to do, or how able He is to do all He plans. Such persons lack purpose in life. Unless they come to know Him through Jesus Christ they will end up lost and without hope. They will be utter failures. In contrast to these we learn through Daniel 11:32: "But the people that do know their God shall be strong, and do exploits." God is looking for such persons according to II Chronicles 16:9: "For the eyes of the Lord run to and fro throughout the whole earth, to show himself strong in the behalf of them whose heart is perfect toward him."

Do we know the Lord in this way? Do we know Him intimately in a deep personal way? This is how Elijah knew Him, and this was one reason why God so abundantly used him.

The prophet's knowledge of God was a growing knowledge. He spent time at the brook of Cherith and there learned to know God intimately. He then spent time in Zarephath where God wonderfully supplied his needs in the home of a poor widow. There again Elijah grew to know God better. This was God's program with Elijah until He called him home to be with Himself.

Paul also teaches us that the knowledge of God should be an ever-increasing matter with us. After stating, "That I may know him, and the power of his resurrection," Paul wrote: "Not as though I had already attained, either were already perfect: but I follow after, if that I may apprehend that for which also I am apprehended of Christ Jesus. Brethren, I count not myself to have apprehended: but this one thing I do, forgetting those things which are behind, and reaching forth unto those things which are before, I press toward the mark for the prize of the high calling of God in Christ Jesus." Let us also press on, for then we will be strong in the power of His might.

Another reason for Elijah's strength was his knowledge of the Divine presence. God was not someone whom he had met on some previous occasion, perhaps in Gilead, perhaps in some mountain hideaway. Instead, He was the Lord God of Israel "before whom I stand," Elijah said. The prophet recognized he was always in the presence of God. The knowledge of this truth has a remarkable effect upon a person's thinking and actions and character.

We who belong to the Lord are always in His presence. He has promised, "I will never leave thee nor forsake thee." We do not see Him with our physical eyes, and we may even be unaware of His presence, but He is with us.

Elijah knew that even while he stood in the presence of King Ahab, he was also standing in the presence of One who was infinitely greater. Since Almighty God was with him, why should he tremble before a worm of this earth?

Our Lord in giving us our instructions said we were to go out into the whole world, and He added this promise: "Lo, I am with you always even unto the end of the age." He sends us out but He goes with us. Wherever we are, He is. This is good to remember when we are tempted to be discouraged or feel that God has stopped answering our prayers and that the heavens are brass. We may not feel His presence; the great essential is to know His presence. Our feelings are but fleeting emotions, they easily come and go; but knowing is based on the Word of God, and that Word is true. Elijah was a strong man of God and a bold witness because he had the consciousness of the Divine presence before him all the time.

A fourth factor with regard to his unique ministry was that he gave out the unchanging Word of God in a constantly changing world. The world has been changing about us in our short lifetime. In fact, some of us have seen in a little more than half a century some of the greatest changes this world has known. These changes include not only the sciences and transportation and communication but religion as well. Man with his philosophies and activities stemming from these philosophies is seeking largely to live without God.

The world does change around us fast, but does it change us with it? Do we tend to give in to the world spirit, compromising our standards in order to be less objectionable to worldly people? We have here no thought of being old-fashioned in dress, of wearing the kind of clothes that perhaps our grandparents wore, but living according to the principles of Christ in every area of our lives.

This may include clothing, however, for our western world customs are sometimes little better than that of the heathen who wear nothing but a loincloth. It is a sad fact that many Christians have grown careless in this area of life.

However, what we are thinking of here is something much deeper, something that has to do with the spiritual qualities that go to the very heart of our being. Are the things of the world occupying our attention to where we neglect our responsibilities to our Lord? Does the television take our time from prayer? Do we follow more closely the world's ideas of things than the standards God has set in His Word?

God has never changed but men do. With regard to the subject of divorce, for example, someone asks: "Are you still holding to the old-fashioned doctrine that says there should be no divorce? Everybody thinks differently than that today." It is true that this is not a popular position. Remember, however, that people differed with our Lord Jesus Christ on this very question. He brought them back to first principles when He reminded them that in the beginning it was not so (Matt. 19:3-6). The Lord has not changed so why should we?

Because the ideas of the world are changing, because its educational systems are changing, because its philosophies are changing, and because western civilization is going back to heathenism in many ways, should Christians follow along and do likewise? Should not we rather be willing to stand alone if necessary for the truth of the Word of God? It is through this that we will show we are real children of God and that Christianity has standards that are genuine and real.

Elijah was the man he was because he was a man of faith. Take the element of faith from him even for a moment and you will find him to be weak, fearful, discouraged and wishing to die. This was his experience after the great victory at Mount Carmel. He was threatened by Jezebel and he fled for his life. Instead of keeping his eyes on God, he wanted to give up. But God was faithful to him and in His unchangeable goodness He encouraged and sustained His servant.

The God whom Elijah worshipped is my God. He has not changed in the centuries since Elijah's day. The God who stopped the rain from falling on Palestine for three and one-half years is my God. The God who sent the rain when He decided it was the right time is my God. The God who sent fire from heaven to consume Elijah's offering on Mount Carmel is my God. He is the same God today as then.

This means that if we believe God and are obedient, we, too, will be effective in our service. The power of the Holy Spirit will be given for us to do what God wants us to do according to the measure of our faith and receptivity. Power belongs to God, and we can be strong in the power of His might.

Paul learned that he could do all things through Christ who strengthened him. The apostle found that where he was weak, when he was trusting in God he was strong. Faith must be tested and matured and God will lead us along as far as we are willing to go with Him. Elijah, being a man like us, had his weak moments, but he faced the trials of faith and came up triumphant.

CHAPTER THREE

ELIJAH AT CHERITH

One of the basic points concerning driving an automobile at night is that one should never over drive the distance that his car lights shine. If the lights shine a hundred yards ahead of the car and the driver can see that far, he should be sure to drive at such a speed that he would be able to safely stop within that distance. There is a basic lesson for us in this with regard to the Christian life, a lesson that shines clearly from the experience of Elijah. We are not to go farther than God plans for us. We are not to go ahead of Him, but to travel one step at a time.

The prophet said as he came before Ahab, "As the Lord God of Israel liveth, before whom I stand, there shall not be dew nor rain these years, but according to my word. And the word of the Lord came to him, saying, Get thee hence, and turn thee eastward, and hide thyself by the brook Cherith, that is before Jordan. And it shall be, that thou shalt drink of the brook; and I have commanded the ravens to feed thee there" (I Kings 17:1-4). As we have previously seen, the drought had been on in Israel for at least six months. Thus it was a dangerous thing for Elijah to stand in the presence of Ahab and tell him who was responsible for the lack of rain. Elijah was not ignorant of the dangers knowing that Jezebel had killed all the prophets of God she could reach, but he obeyed God to the letter. He came before the monarch and gave him God's message. This was as far as Elijah was told to go, but as soon as he had obeyed, God had additional instructions for him.

One Step at a Time

With God obedience always comes first, then He reveals the next step. Too many of us in doing the work of God want to

25

see the end. But that is not trusting God, that is trusting sight.
Faith does not see; it trusts and obeys. There must be first
step "one" and trust in God for the next step. It was when
Elijah had delivered His message to Ahab that the word of
the Lord came to him telling him what his next step was to be.
Tradition has it that this brook ran into the Jordan about 15
miles above Jericho. Its waters came from the mountains of
Ephraim from a spring concealed under a high cliff and shaded
by a dense jungle. It is probable that it was in such a spot as
this that God hid His servant, a place of safety made known
after Elijah's first step of obedience.

As we are obedient and search the Scriptures God will
show us the next step we are to take in our spiritual lives.
This is always God's way of working. When Saul was on his
way to Damascus he suddenly saw a great light. He realized
that he was face to face with the Lord and said, "Lord what
wilt thou have me to do?" The Lord replied, "Go on to Damascus and there it will be told you what you should do."
Saul had to take a step of obedience. He waited three days,
and then the answer came.

When Joshua led the people of Israel into the land, God
assured him: "Every place that the sole of your foot shall
tread upon, that have I given unto you" (Josh. 1:3). This is
what we call the law of appropriation. Every place Joshua's
foot walked upon—every step he took added more of the land
to him and Israel. God was not going to give the Israelites the
land all at once, but only as they appropriated it one step at a
time. It was at the moment the priests entered the Jordan
River that it parted. It was as the Israelites completed their
walking around the city of Jericho that the walls collapsed.
In obedience to God they went forward step by step, and then
God gave them what they needed.

The same is true concerning the manna. It was provided
every morning, six days a week. However, it was provided for
just one day at a time. In the Lord's prayer we are taught to
say, "Give us this day our daily bread." What strength or encouragement we need will be given us, for God has said, "As
thy day, so shall thy strength be." Let us remember that the
Lord's work is done a step at a time.

God Asks Our Absolute Trust

We learn also from Elijah's experience that the servant of God must trust Him absolutely. God told Elijah to go to the Brook Cherith and stay, for He had commanded the ravens to feed him there. At no other place would the ravens feed Elijah but at the Brook Cherith, at the spot designated by God. This raises a question with regard to us. Are we where God wants us? Are the troubles we are undergoing the result of our being out of the will of God? We will always face troubles in this world, but this should not discourage us. God provides grace to help us. Some troubles, however, are caused by our not being in the place where God wants us. Such troubles are remedied only as we obey God.

It was at Cherith that the ravens were to bring Elijah his food. Suppose, however, he had thought he knew a better hiding place and had gone back to some spot in the mountains of Gilead? He could have starved to death, for the ravens had not been commanded to go there. The ravens were told by God to go to the Brook Cherith, by those high cliffs near the Jordan River where a special stream was fed by a spring. It was there God would protect Elijah from Ahab's "blood hounds." It was on the border of the land of Samaria, the very land over which Ahab was king. That was the place God was going to protect His servant.

When Israel was passing through the wilderness the manna fell wherever the pillar of cloud or the pillar of fire led. The needed water was always found when the people followed the guiding hand of God. There was always the providentially provided rock and water when they obeyed.

The great principle covering this is stated in the New Testament in these words: "Seek ye first the kingdom of God, and his righteousness; and all these things shall be added unto you." Let us seek to be in His place of service, doing His bidding, doing His work in His way, and He will take care of the other things for us. "Trust in the Lord with all thine heart; and lean not unto thine own understanding. In all thy ways acknowledge him, and he shall direct thy paths" (Prov. 3:5,6).

Faith Tested

As Elijah stayed by the brook the ravens brought him bread and flesh in the morning and bread and flesh in the evening, and he drank of the waters of the stream. But a time of testing arose, for the brook dried up. It, too, was affected by the lack of rain. Elijah began to experience the results of his own prayer. He undoubtedly knew what would happen when he prayed as he did, but the time the water would stop flowing, he possibly did not know.

Why would God test him like this after having directed him to go to this brook? Why did not God keep this water running in a miraculous way if necessary? An incident in the Gospel of John furnishes us with a very possible answer. "When Jesus then lifted up his eyes, and saw a great company come unto him, he said unto Philip, Whence shall we buy bread, that these may eat? And this he said to prove [try] him: for he himself knew what he would do" (John 6:5,6). God knew what He was going to do with His prophet and it was all for his spiritual well-being. We can picture Elijah living in that great canyon, a beautiful place covered with many trees. Little by little the water in the brook began to recede; after a while the birds left the area and the animals also, for they no longer had water to drink. Elijah probably had to dig a hole in the sand to collect a little water for his personal use.

No doubt he wondered if God would forget him. The tempter, the Devil, is never far away from those who are seeking to do the will of God; he might have tried to bring disquiet to the prophet's soul. Perhaps he tempted Elijah to become discouraged with doing the will of God; or he might have suggested that Elijah go back home because he had sinned and was reaping God's displeasure. Satan might even have encouraged him to formulate his own plans, and to take matters into his own hands, then to ask God to bless those plans.

In Isaiah 28:16 we are told, "He that believeth shall not make haste." Apparently Elijah knew this truth and obeyed it. When the things of life seemingly go wrong, it is well for us to wait upon God and not be in a hurry.

We are admonished in Hebrews 13:5,6: "Let your

conversation be without coveteousness; and be content with such things as ye have: for he hath said, I will never leave thee, nor forsake thee. So that we may boldly say, The Lord is my helpor, and I will not fear what man shall do unto me."

Why did God allow the brook to dry up? One reason may have been to teach Elijah, and us, not to trust in the gifts that God gives, but always to trust in God himself. This is very important. We must keep our eyes upon God, not on things, not on gifts, not on blessings. There is a strong tendency in our own day for some believers to have an experience in the Holy Spirit and then get their eyes off of the Lord and on that experience, on the gift instead of the giver.

The brook of popularity dried up for John the Baptist. Some of his friends came to him and told him that his disciples were beginning to follow Jesus. John's response was that of a servant of God who is fully committed to do his master's will. He said, "He must increase, I must decrease." God tests us so that we will keep our eyes on Him.

It must have been hard for Elijah to sit by the brook and watch it disappear, but God was teaching him to turn his eyes from the failing Cherith to the unfailing God. Then just when the brook dried up completely, the word of the Lord came to him again and told him where to go.

Unbelief sees God *through the circumstances,* just as the ten spies went out, looked at the great walls and giants and said concerning the land of Canaan that they could not take it. But faith puts God between the individual and the circumstances and looks at *the circumstances through Him.*

Goliath was a giant, but when David looked at God and saw how powerful He was, Goliath looked very small. So when faith looks to God instead of the circumstances, the circumstances take on their proper proportion in our eyes. They are small, very small.

Another reason why God tested Elijah's faith at Cherith was that His servant needed this private schooling in order to meet further situations. He was noted for his zeal and for the effectiveness of his prayer life. He had asked God that rain be withheld from Israel, and God had answered his prayer. Since

Elijah was a man of like nature to the rest of us, pride might have begun to show itself. He could easily have begun to gloat over his success in prayer. The Lord knew this whether Elijah did or not and prepared him to meet it.

The Apostle Paul had a similar experience which he describes in II Corinthians: "And lest I should be exalted above measure through the abundance of the revelations, there was given to me a thorn in the flesh, the messenger of Satan to buffet me, lest I should be exalted above measure. For this thing I besought the Lord thrice, that it might depart from me. And he said unto me, My grace is sufficient for thee: for my strength is made perfect in weakness. Most gladly therefore will I rather glory in my infirmities, that the power of Christ may rest upon me. Therefore I take pleasure in infirmities, in reproaches, in necessities, in persecutions, in distresses for Christ's sake: for when I am weak, then am I strong" (12:7-10).

The man whom the Lord uses to perform certain tasks must be a humble man. The self-life rises to the surface very quickly and of it we must all beware. God will not share His glory with any, though in due course, He will honor those who have been faithful to Him.

Before God could use Elijah further, He had to hide him away from the haunts of men in order to train him. So his seclusion was intended to provide more than protection from Ahab's vengeance.

There are many examples of this in Scripture. Joseph, the son of Jacob, was sold as a slave to Egypt, but soon rose to be the most trusted servant in Potiphar's household. God, however, had a larger task for this young Israelite, and in order to prepare him for it, He hid him away in a dungeon. He was placed in jail for a crime he did not commit and was seemingly forgotten. Nevertheless, God was training him for greater things. At the right time Joseph was released from prison to become the Prime Minister of Egypt and the preserver of his own people.

Then there was Moses. He became a great man as the son of Pharaoh's daughter. He was in a position to become ruler of Egypt by reason of his adoption into the royal family. He renounced this position, however, and identified himself with his own people who were a nation of slaves. He presented himself to the Israelites as their deliverer, but he was not ready for the task. God hid him away for 40 years in a desert region and when he was ready, brought him forth to be the great emancipator and leader of Israel.

The same truth is seen in the life of David. He showed great promise even while a young man both as a soldier and as a man who wanted to do the will of God. He first came to Israel's attention when he killed Goliath. Yet, after this great success and some others which followed, God had to hide him in places where he met persecution and testings in order to make him the man He wanted him to be.

If God is going to use any of us, He will have to seclude us in some way or another so that through His own personal dealing He can make us what He desires us to be. When we stay where God wants us, and do as He directs, He obligates Himself to fully sustain us. We need to learn to stay where God puts us until He moves us. It is easy for us to let circumstances move us out of the will of God. Perhaps we are having difficulties making ends meet, or we feel that we are not receiving the income that we should receive for our work. So, we start planning and perhaps scheming to change our way of life and locality, if necessary, in order to get the material things we want. We reason that if we are in the will of God, He will not allow us to suffer financial reverses and that a test in this realm is a clear indication that we should move. This could be the case, but it is not always so. It was not so in Elijah's case. He stayed by the brook and saw it was gradually drying up; but since God had placed him there, he was not going to move until God told him to.

Think also of the instruments God uses at times. With regard to the preservation of Elijah's life, God used ravens. To the Israelite these were unclean birds. They were not to be used as food. The tendency was to avoid them. Nevertheless, God used them, thus showing His absolute sovereignty in His choice of instruments. God does not always choose the person who seemingly has all the potentials needed for great service.

God, in His sovereign purpose, chooses whom He will and what He wills, to do His work.

In feeding Elijah through ravens, God showed His supremacy in the exercise of power. He made good what He had promised. These birds brought food day after day to Elijah even in the days that the brook was drying up. They were under God's direction and never once failed in their appointed task.

Here is what the Psalmist says in this connection: "Whatsoever the Lord pleased, that did he in heaven, and in earth, in the seas, and all deep places" (Ps. 135:6). All nature obeys Him. Do we? Nature has no free will but we do. We ought to be the ones who willingly obey Him since it is our privilege to fellowship with Him. The lower creatures in nature do not have such a privilege; nevertheless, God uses them to perform His will.

In carrying out His purposes, God uses both the natural and the supernatural. In Elijah's case, the brook was a natural means of satisfying the prophet's need for water. At the same time, since Elijah had prayed that God would withhold the rains and the dew from Israel, the brook began to dry up. This was a natural consequence of God's answer to his prayer. On the other hand, the fact that the ravens brought the prophet his food day after day, was a supernatural thing. They were not doing what was normal and usual to their nature. Their feeding of Elijah was a daily miracle.

When the children of Israel escaped from Egypt and traveled to Canaan, God attended their journey with supernatural events and provisions. He gave them manna from heaven, the flesh of birds, and water from rocks. As for their clothing and shoes, these did not wear out while the Israelites lived in the desert. God has His own ways of doing things since He is sovereign. When God calls us to do a work for Him, it is not our business to inquire how He is going to do it. Our responsibility is to obey. It is God's business to choose the method He will use.

It is conceivable that Satan might have tempted Elijah to think that the ravens would eat the food themselves and not bring it to him. There is no record that this took place; but had

Elijah thought such a thing, he would have been putting his faith in the instrument instead of God. His faith, however, was in the Lord and not in the instrument. The Psalmist said, "My heart is fixed." By this, he meant that his trust was in the Lord, and nothing would sway him. We, too, must place our trust in the Creator and not the creature.

The promise of Philippians 4:19 is that God will supply all our needs according to His riches in glory by Christ Jesus. There is no point in us trying to find out how God will do this. Our responsibility is to believe that He will.

ELIJAH AT ZAREPHATH

Because Elijah was a man like us, he undoubtedly wondered what God had in store for him when he saw the brook beginning to dry up. Since he was trusting in God, however, he exemplified what Isaiah says, "He that believeth shall not make haste" (28:16). Elijah believed and help arrived. God did not send a sudden squall of rain for that immediate neighborhood, nor did he provide some supernatural source of water in that place. Instead, "The word of the Lord came unto him, saying, Arise, get thee to Zarephath, which belongeth to Zidon, and dwell there: behold, I have commanded a widow woman there to sustain thee" (I Kings 17:8,9). Elijah was to arise, to go and to dwell in that place. It was at Zarephath only that a widow woman would provide food for him.

Elijah was sent to the country from which Jezebel came, a heathen country where most of the inhabitants worshipped Baal.

The journey was long and hard, for Zidon was some 100 miles from Cherith. Elijah had to travel on foot through many wild and barren places, and this during a great famine. Added was the danger of passing through the country over which Ahab ruled. Nevertheless, Elijah obeyed.

The word Zarephath means "refining" or "a smelting furnace." This land was ruled by Jezebel's father who was a heathen tyrant and a wicked idolator like his daughter. God's purpose in sending Elijah there was to use it in his life for a smelting furnace that would remove the dross of pride or any tendency to self-reliance or independent action apart from Him. The Lord was preparing a cleansed vessel for the next great step in His plan of deliverance and cleansing for Israel.

Elijah arose and went to Zarephath, "and when he came to the gate of the city, behold, the widow woman was there gathering up sticks: and he called to her, and said, Fetch me, I pray thee, a little water in a vessel, that I may drink" (I Kings 17:10). We are not told how many days Elijah traveled, but when he arrived at the city he found the person he was looking for. God always works at both ends of our journey when we move in obedience to Him. He never leaves us in the lurch.

In verse 9 this woman was simply designated as "a widow woman." Her name was not given nor anything more about her. Whether she was rich or poor, a Jewess or a Gentile was not told him. In verse 10 the words are "the widow woman." The definite article indicates that this was the woman God had in mind. She was the only widow who had been commanded of God to provide for His servant.

We can see this, of course, since we have the Bible, and it makes it plain that this was the woman God had in mind. Elijah did not know this at first, but tested her out to see if she was the proper one. He asked her to bring him a little water in a vessel that he might drink. As she went to fetch it, he called to her and said, "Bring me, I pray thee, a morsel of bread in thine hand. And she said, As the Lord thy God liveth, I have not a cake, but an handful of meal in a barrel, and a little oil in a cruse: and, behold, I am gathering two sticks, that I may go in and dress it for me and my son, that we may eat it, and die" (vv. 10-12).

What a prospect faced both the prophet and the widow! She was poor to the point of being destitute. She had no resources except for a handful of meal and a little oil. Yet, God said, "This is the one." This must have been an humbling experience for Elijah to realize that he had been sent to the poorest of the poor in a time of famine and drought to be sustained. Should not God's prophet have the best? This is what people often say concerning the Lord's servants. In reality, Elijah did get the best, for this was God's choice for him. If the prophet had considered the circumstances only, he might have left, but knowing that God must increase and he must decrease, he was obedient and stayed.

The Widow Tested by Elijah

Let us put ourselves in the prophet's position for a moment. He was sent to Zarephath where he was told a widow would take care of him, but he was not told which widow. Undoubtedly, there were many in that place. How was he to find out? He would know of the experience of Abraham's servant when he sought a wife for Isaac. There the test was whether or not the young woman would water the servant's camels without being asked to do so. It was through this that Eliezer found the bride of Isaac. It would seem that Elijah prayed to the Lord in very much the same way.

He put three tests to the widow. First, he requested: "Fetch me, I pray thee, a little water in a vessel, that I may drink." She passed this first test, but Elijah was cautious and added another. The request for water might have been answered in the affirmative by anyone, but the second request would put a different face on the matter. He was doing God's work and seeking God's will and he was not taking any chances, so he asked her if she might bring him a little bread to eat.

Her reply was one of despair and dejection. To a man, however, who remembered how God had sustained Israel in the desert and how God had just recently taken care of him at the Brook Cherith her reply lifted up his spirits. It was faith that spoke when Elijah said, "Fear not; go and do as thou hast said: but make me thereof a little cake first, and bring it unto me, and after make for thee and for thy son." Then he added this promise from God: "For thus saith the Lord God of Israel, The barrel of meal shall not waste, neither shall the cruse of oil fail, until the day that the Lord sendeth rain upon the earth" (I Kings 17:13,14).

On the surface this third test by Elijah may seem selfish. She was to bring him something before she or her son were served. Elijah's motive, however, was very apparent. He was not concerned for himself, for he knew God and knew how God could provide. Elijah was testing the woman's heart. In the words of the New Testament he was finding out if she would seek first the kingdom of God and His righteousness and trust God to add all other things to her.

Faith ventures out and looks for the results to follow. When God commands, it is for us to obey even if what God has said is opposed to what we would call common sense. The circumstances were all against Elijah, the widow and her son, from being sustained in the midst of the famine except that God promised they would be. That was sufficient for Elijah. He knew he had found the woman who was to sustain him until the earth brought forth its fruit again.

Faith goes ahead and trusts God for the results. The priests who carried the ark had to step into the waters of the Jordan before the waters parted. David had to go out into the field and face Goliath before he received the strength to overcome his evil foe.

Man wants to see the end from the beginning, but faith is content to just take what God says. There was not a full barrel of meal, only a little meal in the barrel. But faith saw that small amount as quite sufficient because of God's promises. Elijah had been first sent to a brook where there was water but no food, and yet God supplied. Here at Zarephath there was a little something in the bottom of the barrel. Faith is not occupied with the difficulties but with the Lord with whom all things are possible. Faith is not caught up in the circumstances, but is occupied with the God who controls the circumstances.

A little oil, a little meal and a little water for three persons — and God. That is sufficient. Like Paul, we would declare, "How fathomless the depths of God's resources, wisdom, and knowledge! How unsearchable His decisions, and how mysterious His methods! For who has ever understood the thoughts of the Lord, or has ever been His adviser? Or who has ever advanced God anything to have Him pay him back? For from Him everything comes, through Him everything lives, and for Him everything exists. Glory to Him forever! Amen" (Rom. 11:33-36, Williams).

The Widow Tested by God

Not only did Elijah test this woman to find out if she was the person whom God had selected to provide for him, God also tested her. This He did through Elijah, and the test showed she was a person obedient to God. This Gentile widow living in an environment of Baal worship filled the prophet's request and believed the promise of God that she would not lack food for the duration of the famine. In I Kings 17:15 we see her immediate reaction to Elijah's request: "And she went and did according to the saying of Elijah: and she, and he, and her house, did eat many days." True faith requires obedient action, a requirement which she fulfilled. The result that followed her faith was that her whole household, including her guest, did not lack for food.

This woman went forth in faith and did just as Elijah told her to. This obligated God to fulfill His promise. God delights to honor such faith. He wants to do it, is ready to do it, and is waiting to do it for us. According to verse 16: "The barrel of meal wasted not, neither did the cruse of oil fail, according to the word of the Lord, which he spake by Elijah."

Each passing day these folks in this widow's household had the same test of faith — they scraped the bottom of the barrel. Yet, each day they found sufficient in the barrel to meet their needs for that day. A consistent walk of faith requires walking with God day by day. When such a walk is sustained, God's blessings follow.

Consider again Matthew 6:33: "Seek ye first the kingdom of God, and his righteousness; and all these things shall be added unto you." This is a promise that can be taken in a general way covering the goal of life or it can be considered as a daily promise. In fact, for life's goal to be reached in this fashion it must be lived a day at a time with us seeking first God's kingdom and His righteousness.

In Psalm 34:9 is a promise that has encouraged many of God's people: "O fear the Lord, ye his saints: for there is no want to them that fear him." The word "fear" in this context means "reverential faith or trust." In another Psalm we learn: "No good thing will he withhold from them that walk uprightly" (Ps. 84:11).

Still another promise is found in Proverbs 19:17: "He that hath pity upon the poor lendeth unto the Lord; and that which he hath given will he pay him again."

Sufficient for the Day

Few of us have faced the extremity this widow experienced. It seemed as though each day starvation looked her in the face, yet each day by faith she looked into the face of God. The result was that she and her house "did eat many days." God supplied not a year at a time but a day at a time.

This is what we need with regard to God's grace. We do not need a great stockpile of it for future use, but a daily appropriation of it which God supplies freely. Just as the manna was gathered daily, not in the evening, but in the morning of each day and each one gathered for himself, so must we gather grace from God. We cannot hoard today's grace for tomorrow, or call on yesterday's grace for today. We cannot gather enough on a Sunday to last a whole week. It is good to gather what we can on that day, but we need to have daily contact with God, particularly through the morning watch.

Paul reminds us in II Corinthians 4: "For which cause we faint not; but though our outward man perish, yet the inward man is renewed day by day" (v. 16). If we use what is given, then more will be provided. "As thy day, so shall thy strength be," we are told. Our Saviour instructs us to pray for our daily bread.

Can our cup of joy run over when our cruse of oil has only enough in it for the next day? Do we have a sense of security when the barrel of meal is not full? Where there is only enough for one more day? We talk these days of material security from the cradle to the grave, and all too often our joy depends on our material prosperity. But God was teaching this widow that she could have a cup of joy running over, though she had only oil for another day. She had this security because her eyes did not look at the barrel she would scrape each day but at the God who promised to take care of her needs.

The writer to the Hebrews gives this exhortation: "Let your conversation be without covetousness; and be content with such things as ye have: for he hath said, I will never leave thee, nor forsake thee" (13:5). God does not promise that He will at this moment supply everything we need for the rest of our lives and lay it before us so that we can see it. If we can see it, then it is not a matter of faith but sight. Faith looks to God for strength for the day, food for the day, indeed, all the needs for the day. The life of faith is a step by step walk in conformity to the will and purposes of God.

Perhaps in the case of this widow's household Elijah would come down from his little room in the early morning and together with the widow and her son have morning devotions. They would look to God and encourage themselves in His greatness. Then the widow would go to her barrel and scrape the bottom of it and find sufficient meal for that day. She would take what was needed knowing that because of God's greatness and power, there would be sufficient in the barrel again the following day. She would get the cruse of oil and pour all of the oil out of it; but because she had looked into the face of God she would remember His faithfulness and with confidence trust in Him for the next day's supply.

The Spirit and Power of Elijah

A significant statement is made concerning Elijah in the first chapter of Luke's Gospel. We begin the quotation with verse 15, with John the Baptist as the subject: "For he shall be great in the sight of the Lord, and shall drink neither wine nor strong drink; and he shall be filled with the Holy Ghost, even from his mother's womb. And many of the children of Israel shall he turn to the Lord their God. And he [John the Baptist] shall go before him [Jesus] in the spirit and power of Elias [Elijah], to turn the hearts of the fathers to the children, and the disobedient to the wisdom of the just; to make ready a people prepared for the Lord."

For the Scriptures to say that John the Baptist was to go before the Lord "In the Spirit and power of Elijah" is a testimony to the fact that Elijah was a man of spiritual power. James tells us he was a man of "the same nature as we are," yet he was a man full of the Holy Spirit. In the Old Testament economy, for the Holy Spirit to indwell and control a man as Elijah was indwelt and controlled, was something extra. But in this age, it is the privilege of every born-again believer to be indwelt by the Holy Spirit. In Old Testament times God picked out certain men for specific purposes and empowered them with the Holy Spirit to carry out those purposes. In this age of God's working with men, the Apostle Paul tells us that the believer's body is the temple of the Holy Ghost. He is in us and we are not our own. We are the temple of God, and the Spirit of God dwells in us (I Cor. 6:19,20).

This indwelling of the Spirit is in response to our Lord's prayer recorded in John 14:16,17: "And I will pray the Father, and he shall give you another Comforter, that he may abide with you for ever; Even the Spirit of truth; whom the world cannot receive, because it seeth him not, neither knoweth him: but ye know him; for he dwelleth with you, and shall be in you."

Elijah was responsible to God in a very special way because of being endued with the Spirit of God for a particular work. We not only have the indwelling of the Spirit, but we can have the enduement of the Spirit in order to fulfill the purpose of God in our lives. He will hold us accountable for this at the judgment seat of Christ according to II Corinthians 5. There we will be rewarded for what we have done that pleases God and will lose rewards for what displeases God.

In writing to the Ephesians, Paul declared: "In whom ye also trusted, after that ye heard the word of truth, the gospel of your salvation: in whom also after that ye believed, ye were sealed with that holy Spirit of promise" (1:13,14). The apostle does not say that we were sealed "by" the Holy Spirit, which would make the Holy Spirit the instrument of our sealing. Rather he says we were sealed "with" the Holy Spirit which means that the Holy Spirit is our Seal. He is the Earnest of our inheritance. He has been given to us until the redemption of the purchased possession. The moment we became children of God, the Holy Spirit took up His abode in us. But in order for us to be filled with the Holy Spirit, we must give Him possession of every aspect of our lives. He must control every phase of our being.

From the life of Elijah we learn that there are three simple conditions to being controlled by the Holy Spirit.

Empty of Self

First of all, we must be empty of self. God cannot fill us if we are already filled with the self-life. Elijah was emptied of self during that long period of three and one-half years of drought and waiting on God. First his experiences at the Brook Cherith and later at Zarephath taught him that he could do nothing of himself. He could not so much as provide food for himself. Even water, one of the most common commodities of life was possible to him only through God's provision.

It was in proportion to his being emptied of self and of self-sufficiency and self-dependence that he was filled with the Holy Spirit of power. So, while Elijah waited on the time when God would deal in this very specific way with Israel, the Holy Spirit was taking more and more possession of him. Later, of course, there was the great triumph at Mount Carmel, but that triumph was not possible until God had full possession of His servant.

There are some people who seek more of the Holy Spirit, but this is wrong. They have this matter turned around. The Holy Spirit is seeking more of us. He already indwells each believer. For us to have His fullness does not mean that we should seek more of Him but that He be given control of all areas of our lives. It is a serious matter to put the cart before the horse on this subject.

Some people look within themselves for evidence of His indwelling and refuse to believe in His presence unless they can detect some symptom or sign that they think should be present. This is also wrong. The Scriptures make it plain that we are indwelt by the Spirit the moment we receive Christ as our Saviour. This we accept by faith. He will take complete control of our lives as we fulfill the three conditions seen in Elijah's experience, the first of which is that we must be empty of self.

In one of his great discourses our Lord said, "If any man thirst, let him come unto me, and drink...this spake he of the Spirit" (John 7:37-39). If we thirst for the filling of the Holy Spirit then Christ will fill us. We do not drink when we are already full, but only when we are thirsty. We drink when there is a need. We must recognize the emptiness of self before we can drink of His fullness. The Lord's promise is, "He that believeth on me as the Scripture hath said, out of his innermost being shall flow rivers of living water."

The evidence, then, of the Spirit's presence in us does not lie in signs but is accepted on the basis of faith. I accept what God says and that settles it. The Holy Spirit does not make Himself known to us by signs pointing to Himself, for He reveals not Himself, but Christ: "Howbeit when he, the Spirit of truth, is come, he will guide you into all truth: for he shall not speak of himself; but whatsoever he shall hear, that shall he speak: and he will show you things to come. He shall glorify me: for he shall receive of mine, and shall show it unto you" (John 16:13,14).

One of the surest indications of the presence of the indwelling Spirit is sensitiveness to sin. It is a sad commentary on professing believers that many of them talk about the fullness of the Holy Spirit in their lives, yet they evidence cantankerousness and argumentativeness which are works of the flesh and not fruit of the Spirit. Tenderness of conscience is another evidence of the Spirit's presence. There is also the increasing preciousness of Christ, and sympathy with His purposes in the world and in our own hearts.

Obedience

The second condition for the fullness of the Holy Spirit is obedience. When God told Elijah he must go to a certain place, he went. Some of the conditions may have seemed extreme, but he did not question them. He did as God said. For example, it was an exceedingly dangerous step for Elijah to take when he entered the presence of Ahab. Yet, God had said, "Go show thyself to Ahab," and Elijah did.

It was rather an odd thing for God to tell him to go and hide himself at the Brook Cherith and he would find food and water there but this he did also. Then, when the brook dried up, God told him to go to Zarephath and there he would find a widow who would sustain him. Elijah obeyed and found God's promises to be fulfilled to the letter. Later, when God decided it was time to send rain, He told him to show himself to Ahab the second time. Elijah did this without hesitating. The point is that he was obedient to whatever God told him to do.

We grow in fullness only as we continue in obedience. The Holy Spirit's fullness is given only for the fulfilling of God's purposes. God will not give us the fullness of the Spirit save only for the complete realization of His will in our lives. We must be subject to His directions and plans without reservation.

Live on the Word

The third condition is that we must live on the Word of God. The Holy Spirit works through the Word of God. Only as we feed on it day by day, do we meet God's conditions.

Our Saviour said in John 6: "As the living Father hath sent me, and I live by the Father: so that he that eateth me, even he shall live by me. This is that bread which came down from heaven: not as your fathers did eat manna, and are dead: he that eateth of this bread shall live for ever" (vv. 57,58). A little later in the chapter He explained that eating His flesh meant obeying His Word. He said, "It is the spirit that quickeneth; the flesh profiteth nothing: the words that I speak unto you, they are spirit, and they are life" (v. 63). So the third way to the fullness of the Spirit is to let the Word of God have full reign in our hearts.

A neglected Bible means a starved and strengthless spirit. It means a barren life, and the Spirit of God is grieved by such barrenness. Many people run to meetings for crumbs of help but do not search and meditate on the Word of God for themselves. Let us learn to make the Word the man of our counsel.

We meet the conditions of the filling of the Spirit when we are emptied of self, are obedient to what God directs, and feed constantly on the Word of God. This is the way to power. Let us follow the admonition of the Psalmist who says, "But his delight is in the law of the Lord; and in his law doth he meditate day and night. And he shall be like a tree planted by the rivers of water, that bringeth forth his fruit in his season; and his leaf also shall not wither; and whatsoever he doeth shall prosper" (Ps. 1:2,3).

Elijah's Private Life Put to the Test

Did Elijah have strings on God? Can He do for us what He did for Elijah? Was He just the God of Elijah, or is Elijah's God our God? These are not idle questions but go to the very heart of the significance of these Scripture passages we have been studying.

Elijah was thoroughly tested in both his public and private life. Sometimes we can make impressions as believers in public that are much better than our conduct in private. How do we act when the toast is burned, or the steak is overcooked? How do we respond when cherished plans are altered by circumstances? Perhaps someone comes to us for help or a family condition arises that needs attention—how do we respond to these things? Persons who are filled with the Holy Spirit will be the same persons in public and in private. The Spirit-controlled man exhibits the fruit of the Spirit anywhere he happens to be.

The 17th verse of I Kings 17 says, "And it came to pass after these things, that the son of the woman, the mistress of the house, fell sick; and his sickness was so sore, that there was no breath left in him. And she said unto Elijah, What have I to do with thee, O thou man of God? art thou come unto me' to call my sin to remembrance, and to slay my son?" We can think of extenuating circumstances for this mother who was bereft of her son. She had possibly been tending him night and day as he lay on his sick bed, and her nerves were strained to the breaking point. She spoke unadvisedly and cruelly to this good man who had brought to her home nothing but kindness and the blessings of God.

Elijah might have been trapped into giving a quick and sharp answer. After all, he was innocent of the accusation she made. However, in spite of the provocation, he did not lose his poise.

The death of her son reminded the widow of some past sin, apparently. Her conscience was aroused and she wanted to vindicate her character in her own eyes. Under such circumstances a person wants to turn the blame, if there is any, on someone else.

We realize that she very likely had a heathen background and had been a worshipper of Baal. It is possible that by this time she was a believer in the true God, but the death of her son had been a great shock to her. Her conscience for some reason or another was aroused, and our consciences can make us very uncomfortable.

Without a doubt Elijah's holy life had brought conviction of sin upon her. This can happen to any of us. Sometimes this conviction comes from a member of our own family, a child perhaps, or a wife and mother whose good life makes others in the home aware of their evil ways. Joseph's brothers were convicted of their past mistreatment of him when they met trouble in Egypt.

It may have been that the Lord was trying to do something special for this woman because the Word says, "Whom the Lord loveth he chasteneth, and scourgeth every son whom he receiveth" (Heb. 12:6). At the time these things take place in our lives it is not easy for us to understand the reason for them.

Perhaps our reaction to some sorrow or loss or problem is, "Do I deserve this?" Or "Why has God treated me so harshly?" If we have lost a loved one, perhaps we ask why God took that loved one; and if it is a child, perhaps we will say, "Why did God punish my little child?" We wonder why we have to suffer and our neighbors go scot-free. This is the carnal man expressing himself, not the spiritual man.

See how Elijah met this difficult situation: "And he said unto her, Give me thy son. And he took him out of her bosom, and carried him up into a loft, where he abode, and laid him upon his own bed." What a gentle answer this was that Elijah gave. He had been falsely accused and that not by a stranger, for he had been dwelling in the home of the widow for quite some time. It is true they did not have an abundance of things but they were not starving. They had little variety in their food, but they were eating twice a day at least and had water to drink. In a time of famine they had a sufficiency, and they had been going through this together. The fruit of the Spirit was seen in Elijah's response – love, joy, peace, longsuffering, gentleness, goodness, meekness, faith. Elijah was in private the same kind of man he was in public.

Love according to I Corinthians 13 "suffereth long." It is kind, it is not easily provoked and it bears all things and endures all things. Perhaps some will say this was all right for Elijah because he was a man specially endued with the Spirit of God. He was that, it is true; but he was also a man of like passions as we are. He had the same old nature we have and he had to contend with it at all times. It was not dead though potentially it was crucified. Paul says, "I am crucified with Christ: nevertheless I live; yet not I, but Christ liveth in me: and the life which I now live in the flesh I live by the faith of the Son of God, who loved me, and gave himself for me" (Gal. 2:20). The Holy Spirit is the only Person who could produce this kind of fruit in a life.

We are no different than Elijah in this respect; and the same Spirit who indwells us indwelt Elijah and can do for us what He did for him. Elijah responded to the Spirit's dealing in his life and gave himself over completely to Him. Elijah knew that if God was to use him to the full he would have to walk close with Him.

I talked one day with a man whom God was mightily using and asked him about his devotional life. He pointed to the door of the room and said, "Brother Epp, I am convinced that if I walk out of that door without having my proper relationship with God attended to in the morning, before the day's responsibilities begin, God would kill me as I passed through the door." The need of a close walk with God was deep in this man's consciousness.

A habit that has blessed my own life is that when I am through working in my study, located in the basement of my home, that I pause before leaving it and ask myself this question: "Am I ready to go out in service?" I stand before the Lord, review my spiritual condition and ask myself if I am going out in His name. Many times I have said, "Lord, I will not go unless You bless me in a special way. I cannot go unless You touch me with Your Spirit in a very definite way. I want to fulfill Your business in a way that is right, and say things in a

spirit and power in which You want them said. I cannot go
without the consciousness of Your unction upon me." I have
then left my study with the consciousness of God's presence
with me and the assurance of His using me.

Elijah was a man who had spent much time in the presence of the Lord and the death of this young lad and the unfair
accusation by his distraught mother did not affect his spiritual
poise. He took the boy in his arms and prayed, "O Lord my God,
hast thou also brought evil upon the widow with whom I so-
journ, by slaying her son?" The Lord had sent him to
that widow's home, and she had graciously taken care of him
for many months, possibly a year or more by then. Elijah, like
us, wondered why God had permitted this to happen. Then, we
are told: "He stretched himself upon the child three times, and
cried unto the Lord, and said, O Lord my God, I pray thee, let
this child's soul come into him again."

This was a prayer of faith concerning which James speaks
in the fifth chapter of his book: "And the prayer of faith shall
save the sick." Where does faith of this nature come from?
From the Word of God and through the Word of God as God
speaks to our hearts. It is clear that Elijah fully believed that
God would answer his prayer. He did not do this in a public
gathering, for there are great matters we discuss with God that
are best done by going to Him alone. There are things that are
accomplished only as we wrestle privately in prayer.

Elijah showed perseverence. He did not give up, but
stretched himself upon the child three times. We are inclined
to give up too soon. We ask God once or perhaps twice, and
then, because we receive no answer, we stop asking. The Lord
Jesus admonished us to be importunate in our praying. When
a thing is of God we should keep on asking.

As we stop to consider this matter a little more we realize
that Elijah was asking for something that had not been previously recorded in all human history. There is no record of
God having raised someone from the dead from the time of
Adam to the time Elijah prayed for the widow's son. Perhaps
he caught the truth from Abraham's prayer concerning Isaac,
for Abraham most certainly believed in the God of the

resurrection. But whatever the source, Elijah was asking for something new in human experience. But he could ask this because he knew God. Ephesians 3:20 says, "But now unto him that is able to do exceeding abundantly above all that we ask or think, according to the power that worketh in us." This was evidently Elijah's concept of God's power. Then he prayed with perseverance. He prayed in faith, nothing wavering, for the person who wavers cannot expect his prayer to be answered.

The Word tells us that the eyes of the Lord are over the righteous and His ears are open to their prayers (I Pet. 3:12). In many instances the Lord is waiting on us to do some real praying. This is what Elijah did.

His one purpose in bringing back this young boy to life was to honor God. The Psalmist says, "Delight thyself also in the Lord; and he shall give thee the desires of thine heart" (Ps. 37:4). Elijah knew this Psalm and undoubtedly read it again and again. The God who could give new life to Israel could easily give new life to this lad.

Life flowed into that youthful body again, and Elijah put the boy in his mother's arms. She said, "Now by this I know that thou art a man of God, and that the word of the Lord in thy mouth is truth." Perhaps others could say that of us if we would but trust God and obey Him, showing the same spirit of trust and submission as this prophet of old.

CHAPTER FIVE

ELIJAH APPROACHES THE DAY OF HIS TRIUMPH

Three and a half years went by before word came to the prophet that the end of the famine was in sight. "And it came to pass after many days, that the word of the Lord came to Elijah in the third year, saying, Go, show thyself unto Ahab; and I will send rain upon the earth. And Elijah went to show himself unto Ahab. And there was a sore famine in Samaria" (I Kings 18:1,2). The moment of Elijah's triumph was fast approaching.

We cannot help but compare the experience of our Lord as He faced the cross with the experience of Elijah as he faced Ahab who would gladly have taken his life. In John 17:1 we read: "These words spake Jesus, and lifted up his eyes to heaven, and said, Father, the hour is come; glorify thy Son, that thy Son also may glorify thee." Our Lord looked to the cross as His coronation day, His day of triumph and day of victory. Elijah was in danger of his life, looking as it were into the lion's mouth in approaching Ahab after three and a half years of famine.

The prophet followed the principle laid down by our Lord many years later when He said, "Except a corn of wheat fall into the ground and die, it abideth alone: but if it die, it bringeth forth much fruit. He that loveth his life shall lose it; and he that hateth his life in this world shall keep it unto life eternal." This was the test Elijah faced, a test which he passed triumphantly because he did not love his life unto death. He would gladly have given his life if it would have brought glory to the Lord.

51

Some years before this God had said to Elijah: "Go hide thyself." He needed to be hidden away in order to spend time with God as well as to be protected from the vindictive Ahab. Elijah's public work needed to be laid aside for the time in order that he might be shut in with God. This was necessary so that the day of glory would be just that—a day of triumph and victory.

Elijah was a man of obedience. When God said to him: "Go hide thyself," and sent him to the Brook Cherith, Elijah went. There he had water to drink and ravens to feed him. When the brook dried up, God said to him: "Arise, get thee to Zarephath . . . I have commanded a widow woman there to sustain thee." Again he obeyed and was blessed in his obedience. The third command was "Go, shew thyself unto Ahab," and with that the promise: "I will send rain upon the earth." In each case there was a command and a promise. As the command was obeyed the promise was fulfilled. Elijah met the condition of obedience promptly in each case.

Obedience to the instructions of God is an act of faith that causes the person involved to trust completely in the Lord and to commit himself entirely into His hands. It is the complete committal of the human will and purpose into the keeping of a Sovereign God. "Commit thy way unto the Lord; trust also in him; and he shall bring it to pass." All this is included in obedience.

No greater illustration of obedience to God is to be found than that of our Lord himself when He said, "My meat is to do the will of him that sent me" (John 4:34). Elijah had learned the Master's secret, and that was to listen to the Word. This is why it took time and why it was necessary to hide himself from the usual haunts of men. He had also learned that he must believe the Word, and that believing it was shown by acting on it. Hearing it was first, and believing it was next. Then, when he obeyed the Word, the results God promised followed automatically.

Life for us is also a life of faith. Paul stated in Galatians 2:20: "I am crucified with Christ: nevertheless I live; yet not I, but Christ liveth in me: and the life which I now live in the flesh I live by the faith of the Son of God, who loved me, and gave himself for me." To the Philippians he said, "Wherefore, my beloved, as ye have always obeyed, not as in my presence only, but now much more in my absence, work out your own salvation with fear and trembling. For it is God which worketh in you both to will and to do of his good pleasure." If we will commit ourselves to the Lord completely and without reservation, He will work in us in such a way that His purposes will be fulfilled in our lives. He works in us to will and to do of His good pleasure; but between the willing and the doing He waits upon our definite committal to Him. He needs our consent; with that His sovereign power goes into operation to carry out His purposes.

That is why Paul could say in another place: "I can do all things through Christ which strengtheneth me." It was Christ in him who caused Paul to want to do the things of God, and then, as he consented to do those things, Christ worked through him.

Elijah had learned that in himself he was nothing. It was possible for God to work through him only as he committed himself to Him. He was a man of like passions as we are. God used him because he was willing to be used by God.

Perhaps we wonder why we are not used as was Elijah. It could be that we refuse the tests Elijah faced and passed. When these tests come we murmur. This keeps us from learning the real secret of Christ's indwelling grace and power. Like Israel of old when we are tried, we complain. We may quote Romans 8:28,29 but we do not believe it. That passage says, "We know that all things work together for good to them that love God, to them who are the called according to his purpose. For whom he did foreknow, he also did predestinate to be conformed to the image of his Son, that he might be the firstborn among many brethren." God's great purpose is to conform us to the image of His Son. If, however, we do not believe He is working out these things in us and are not submitting ourselves to the tests and trials that come upon us, then we cannot be used as was Elijah. He passed through many severe trials, but he yielded himself to God in these experiences and God filled him with His Holy Spirit.

John the Baptist can teach us the secret that is involved here. He said, speaking of Christ: "He must increase, but I must decrease" (John 3:30). Compare for a moment the Lord Jesus to the sun, and John the Baptist to the morning star. Before the sun breaks over the horizon the morning star shines out clear and bright. As the daylight begins to increase, however, the light of the star begins to disappear until it is completely lost sight of altogether. The star is still in the heavens, but the sun so outshines it that we cannot see it.

We speak of sanctification, but what is sanctification in the daily life but Christ increasing in us and the old self-life decreasing? Our own aims and ambitions and high estimate of ourselves become less and less and Christ means more and more.

This was the kind of spiritual growth that Elijah had passed through in those years from the time he started to pray for God's vindication before Israel until the time God said to him: "Go shew thyself unto Ahab." Elijah was obedient because he knew his God. Had he conferred with flesh and blood, he might have been persuaded that he was like a lone swimmer plunging into a raging sea, or an unarmed man walking into a lion's den. He had to present himself before a wicked, idolatrous king, a tyrant, a man armed with despotic power, whose personal enmity against God's prophet had been on the increase for the last three and a half years.

During all this time Ahab had sought by every means possible to find Elijah and arrest him. He had thoroughly searched his own country, as well as all the countries bordering Israel and had taken oaths from them that Elijah was not among them. Thus, it was plain Elijah was to face a vindictive man; but God never asks us to do what is above human nature without imparting sufficient grace and strength for the purpose.

In his first meeting with Ahab, Elijah had told him that there would be no dew or rain except as Elijah prayed for it. Now rain was promised, for God had said it would come. It was necessary for Elijah to announce this fact or the priests of

Baal would, undoubtedly, have claimed that their idol was responsible for the breaking of the long drought. So, in order that God's glory might be maintained and Baal completely confounded, Elijah had to be the instrument through which God would send the rain.

It is very possible that Elijah was comforted by one of David's Psalms written at a time when danger threatened and God delivered him. It begins: "The Lord is my light and my salvation; whom shall I fear? the Lord is the strength of my life; of whom shall I be afraid? When the wicked, even mine enemies and my foes, came upon me to eat up my flesh, they stumbled and fell. Though an host should encamp against me, my heart shall not fear: though war should rise against me, in this will I be confident. . . . For in the time of trouble he shall hide me in his pavilion: in the secret of his tabernacle shall he hide me; he shall set me up upon a rock" (27: 1-3,5).

Still realizing that he walked a dangerous road, David prayed beginning with verse 11: "Teach me thy way, O Lord, and lead me in a plain path, because of mine enemies. Deliver me not over unto the will of mine enemies: for false witnesses are risen up against me, and such as breathe out cruelty. I had fainted, unless I had believed to see the goodness of the Lord in the land of the living." His final admonition is, "Wait on the Lord: be of good courage, and he shall strengthen thine heart: wait, I say, on the Lord" (v. 14).

Elijah Meets Obadiah

As Elijah, in obedience to God's command, set out to meet Ahab, he saw that the famine was very severe in Samaria. Apparently it extended beyond the borders of Israel, but Samaria seemed to be getting the brunt of it. This, of course, was in line with God's judgment, because it was His people He was disciplining. The Prophet Isaiah wrote, "If ye be willing and obedient, ye shall eat the good of the land: But if ye refuse and rebel, ye shall be devoured with the sword: for the mouth of the Lord hath spoken it" (1:19,20). This principle was literally fulfilled before Elijah's eyes. The people had rebelled and they were not eating of the good of the land. It is very likely that a large number of Israelites had died of starvation. The widow who took care of Elijah was on the verge of starvation when God sent him to her home for her to be the sustainer of his physical life.

Obedience to God is the key to His blessings upon us. Israel had suffered for three and a half years because of dis- obedience, but now because of the obedience of a man of God, the Lord's judgment would be lifted.

The first man Elijah met, however, was not Ahab, but Obadiah, the governor of Ahab's household. This is how it came about: "And Ahab called Obadiah, which was the gov- ernor of his house. (Now Obadiah feared the Lord greatly: For it was so, when Jezebel cut off the prophets of the Lord, that Obadiah took a hundred prophets, and hid them by fifty in a cave, and fed them with bread and water.) And Ahab said unto Obadiah, Go into the land, unto all fountains of water, and unto all brooks: peradventure we may find grass to save the horses and mules alive, that we lose not all the beasts. So they divided the land between them to pass throughout it: Ahab went one way by himself, and Obadiah went another way by himself" (I Kings 18:3-6).

All that we know about Obadiah is given to us in this chapter. His life, like that of Elijah's, is very instructive for us. The men are not necessarily on the same spiritual level, but Obadiah was a God-fearing man, a believer, holding a very influential position at the seat of power in Samaria. He was in a position to know the terrible inroads that the worship of Baal had made in the kingdom. God had his men in high places in government before this time and after. Joseph was prime minister in Egypt, Daniel was high in the government under Nebuchadnezzar, and Nehemiah was cupbearer to Artaxerxes. Obadiah was not uncompromising like Daniel, however. Everyone knew where Daniel stood or Nehemiah or Ezra or some of the others, but Obadiah apparently was not as clear cut in his position.

God said, however, that Obadiah was a believer though he apparently had no influence in raising the spiritual tone of Ahab's life. Daniel had his enemies in court, but he also had a profound affect upon the monarchs under whom he served. Undoubtedly, Obadiah was greatly shocked when he saw how Jezebel killed the prophets of God, and his conduct in preserving a number of them alive is highly commendable.

One thing Obadiah evidently did not do, he did not rebuke sin. He may have been like some of God's people today who say, "Don't carry this thing too far. Say just as little as is necessary to get by." Perhaps he thought his presence would influence Ahab, but it is clear that he did not get very far. He did not live the life of a separated man standing out for the truth of God as some of the others did. He was satisfied with being defensive concerning his faith, but he was not aggressive in witnessing to it. He was not all out in promoting the cause of God.

God used him and records no criticism of him. God simply paints the picture before us so that we can see the man Obadiah was. However, it is clear from II Corinthians 6 what the believer's position should be in the midst of idolatry and unbelief: "Be ye not unequally yoked together with unbelievers: for what fellowship hath righteousness with unrighteousness? and what communion hath light with darkness? And what concord hath Christ with Belial? or what part hath he that believeth with an infidel?"

Then the admonition is given for the believer to separate, for the Scripture continues: "Wherefore, come out from among them, and be ye separate, saith the Lord, and touch not the unclean thing; and I will receive you, And will be a Father unto you, and ye shall be my sons and daughters, saith the Lord Almighty. Having therefore these promises, dearly beloved, let us cleanse ourselves from all filthiness of the flesh and spirit, perfecting holiness in the fear of God" (I Cor. 6:17-7:1). This is the great principle so much needed to be obeyed today.

In the Book of Hebrews the same truth is taught in 13:13: "Let us go forth therefore unto him [Christ] without the camp, bearing his reproach. For here have we no continuing city, but we seek one to come." This apparently was not the attitude of Obadiah's heart.

We find in II Timothy 2:21 another principle: "If a man therefore purge himself from these, he shall be a vessel unto

honour, sanctified, and meet for the master's use, and prepared unto every good work." Obadiah had done some good
things, but his compromising left him unprepared to be used as
fully as God would like to have used him.

Elijah stands in contrast to all this. He was not a great
man as the world would count men great. He was not the prime
minister of a powerful nation, nor did he hold the position that
Obadiah held in the house of Ahab. Elijah belonged more in
the category that Paul describes in I Corinthians 1:26-29
where we are told that God did not choose many mighty nor
many wise, but mostly the weak and the despised to do His
work. He chose some of the others such as Daniel and Paul, but
usually, He calls not the great, but the ordinary.

Obadiah held a position of prestige and influence in over-
seeing Ahab's household and by having charge of all his many
possessions. But instead of him lifting up Ahab, apparently
Ahab tended to drag Obadiah down to where he was concerned
more about cattle and herds and possessions than about the
will of God.

Does this speak to our hearts? Perhaps to teach us this
lesson is why God allowed this man's life to be included in
the Scriptures.

Ahab and Obadiah had divided the land between them in
their search for pasture for the animals, and it was while
Obadiah was in the way that Elijah met him. He greeted the
prophet with these words: "Art thou that my lord Elijah?"

Obadiah's Fear

Elijah commissioned Obadiah to tell Ahab that he was
looking for him. Obadiah's response was one of fear. He said,
"What have I sinned, that thou wouldest deliver thy servant
into the hand of Ahab, to slay me?" This man lacked moral
strength and spiritual backbone. He lacked vigorous qualities
of spiritual life so that when the commission was given him,
he was reluctant to obey. Back of all this, of course, was lack
of faith, and this could possibly be traced to the fact that he
did not spend much time alone with God. For him to carry word
to Ahab that he had met Elijah and yet had not arrested him

could have brought Ahab's wrath down upon his head. But Elijah's commission was God's commission and Obadiah finally accepted it as such and carried the message to his master.

It was fear that proved disastrous to Peter when he was walking on the water. He did well until he took his eyes off the Lord and looked at the waves. So it was with Obadiah who looked at the circumstances around him instead of trusting God.

Obadiah was the kind of man who recognized the possibilities of God's power, but like many of us he did not see it as something for himself. The great things God could do were for somebody else not for him. Before he agreed to tell Ahab that he had met Elijah he had to be assured that Elijah would stay where Ahab could find him. Obadiah did not want Ahab's wrath to fall on his head. This is why he said, "And it shall come to pass, as soon as I am gone from thee, that the Spirit of the Lord shall carry thee whither I know not; and so when I come and tell Ahab, and he cannot find thee, he shall slay me" (I Kings 18:12).

Then Obadiah went on to vindicate himself in Elijah's eyes. He said, "But I thy servant fear the Lord from my youth. Was it not told my lord what I did when Jezebel slew the prophets of the Lord, how I hid an hundred men of the Lord's prophets by fifty in a cave, and fed them with bread and water?" (vv. 12,13). Obadiah did here what many of us are doing today, namely pointing to statistics as proof of our faithfulness to God. Obadiah gave the number of the prophets he had helped and indicated the amount of food he had provided, yet while he was doing it, he was afraid to be Elijah's messenger to Ahab.

The similarities between Obadiah and Elijah are few and the contrasts many. They were both God-fearing men and both had a commission. Elijah had a commission to show himself to Ahab and Obadiah had a commission to tell Ahab that Elijah was coming. But this is about as far as their likenesses went.

Contrasts Between Elijah and Obadiah

They contrasted greatly with regard to obedience. When God told Elijah to do something, he did it without hesitation. Obadiah, on the other hand, hesitated, fearing for his life. He lacked faith in the power of God. Elijah never questioned for a moment that God would provide the power needed for his commission. Obadiah believed God had such power, but it was not power that he believed was for him personally.

Elijah was a man of great courage. Boldness marked his life. Obadiah, was the opposite. He was a man of fear for the simple reason that through lack of communion and fellowship with God he did not know of the power of God available for him.

Elijah was not one who worried about his reputation. When he was on Mount Carmel he staked his whole reputation on his belief that God would answer by fire. Obadiah was distressed as soon as he heard Elijah commission him and went on the defensive, trying to build up his own reputation by telling what he had done at a previous time.

Elijah had a positive message. He asked his nation why they halted between two opinions. He knew that whoever was not for God was against Him and whoever did not gather with Him scattered abroad. Obadiah was more yielding. He wanted to go along with the crowd as far as he could. He did good things such as feeding the Lord's prophets, but apparently he was not convicted of his sins of omission which were not small.

As to results, Elijah was a man who prevailed on God to act. Fire fell from heaven demonstrating the faithfulness of God. Rain came as God had promised. But as for Obadiah, he was a spectator of these things. Without a doubt he was glad to see God vindicated and rejoiced that Baal had been discredited, but he personally had no part in the results. Let us not overlook the fact that we too can make Obadiah's mistake. We can rejoice that God is working through others, but why not have the joy of Elijah in seeing God working through us? Elijah was a man of like passions as we are, and it is God's desire to accomplish His purposes through His children.

There is one great contrast that grows out of these others. There will be a vast difference in rewards coming to these two men. Elijah was recognized as one of God's greatest men. He was even taken to heaven without dying, and he is to return to prepare the world for Christ's return. He was a man whom God could depend on. It was no wonder that he has been entrusted with the greatest task a man could perform just prior to the Lord's own personal return to this world. As far as Obadiah is concerned, he is not heard of again outside of this one chapter in Scripture.

Why not check our own lives against the lives of these two men. Where do we stand? We may not be as far off as Obadiah was and we may not be as close as Elijah was. The question is, are we where God wants us? Is God able to do things through us, or are we rejoicing only in the things God is doing through others? It is those who know God that are strong and can do exploits. Let us learn to know Him. Let us take time to do so, for this knowledge does not come overnight. Time spent in the presence of God brings eternal results.

A View of Ahab's Character

We have already seen Ahab to be an infidel, a blasphemer, even though he was king of the ten tribes of Israel. So far as his home life is concerned he might be described as a "henpecked" husband. It is apparent that his strong-minded wife, Jezebel, ran his life. We have already seen that she imposed her religion on her husband and his kingdom.

Ahab gave the following instructions to Obadiah: "Go into the land, unto all the fountains of water, and unto all the brooks: peradventure we may find grass to save the horses and mules alive, that we lose not all the beasts. So they divided the land between them to pass throughout it: Ahab went one way by himself, and Obadiah went another way by himself" (I Kings 18:5,6).

While Elijah was on his way to see Ahab, the king had also set out on a journey. Elijah was on an errand for the honor of God, the God of Israel. Ahab was searching for food for his cattle, horses and mules. He had no concern about God. In spite of the fact that the country had seen three and a half years of famine and he knew that his sin and that of his household and Israel's apostasy had brought this upon his kingdom, he still had no concern for his own sin and no thought of repentance toward God. A relief from the Divine judgment was all that he thought about or cared about; he made no attempt to remedy the situation that had brought the judgment to begin with. He was very much like Pharaoh who, when a plague struck, called for Moses and asked Moses to pray to remove the plague. Then, once the judgment was removed, Pharaoh returned to his former evil ways.

This is characteristic of unregenerate men. We read in Revelation 16: "And the fifth angel poured out his vial upon the seat of the beast; and his kingdom was full of darkness; and they gnawed their tongues for pain, And blasphemed the God of heaven because of their pains and their sores, and repented not of their deeds" (vv. 10,11).

One would think that Ahab being king of Israel would have been concerned about his people ahead of his animals. Such was not the case, however. By shutting God out of first place, Ahab's evil heart seemed incapable of rising any higher than concern for his horses and mules.

How different this was from David, a man after the heart of God. When he saw the judgment of God about to fall on Israel because of his own personal sin, he pleaded that his people might be spared and that he be punished, for he not they did the evil (II Sam. 24:17).

We are living in days of danger and judgment. We pray for revival, but why? Is it in order that the character of the days might change? Do we want God to halt the onslaughts of evil forces for His glory or for our comfort? Elijah wanted to see God honored before all the nation, but Ahab sought only relief from the results of the drought.

This was the man who met Elijah in the way. Ahab was so infuriated against the prophet of God that he had sought him everywhere. Instead of looking at his own evil deeds Ahab had considered Elijah to be the cause of all his trouble and the worst enemy of his nation. Ahab wanted to destroy him, but he first had to find him. He could not locate Elijah anywhere in Samaria, and his search throughout the neighboring countries ended with the same result. Elijah was not to be found.

Holy Boldness

It was with holy boldness that Elijah met this merciless and despotic ruler. He was willing to give his physical life for the honor and glory of God.

At a later time, Paul the Apostle, when warned that if he went to Jerusalem he would have nothing but trouble, gave this answer: "But none of these things move me, neither count I my life dear unto myself, so that I might finish my course with joy, and the ministry, which I have received of the Lord Jesus, to testify the gospel of the grace of God" (Acts 20:24). Paul had one task to fulfill and that he was determined to do.

At another place when warned again of what was before him, Paul answered: "What mean ye to weep and to break mine heart? for I am ready not to be bound only, but also to die at Jerusalem for the name of the Lord Jesus" (Acts 21:13). Surely things would begin to happen if we had this kind of love and devotion to Christ! This was the heart attitude that characterized Elijah. His greatest aim was to let it be known that God was God in Israel. He was God's servant and cared only for the mind and will of God. Elijah was God's bondslave, and a slave does not originate his own plans.

How do we fit into this type of wholehearted devotion to the Lord? Is our eagerness for the success of our work or our church or our sect only. If these thrive, are we satisfied? If these do not thrive, do we become depressed?

Once a man is satisfied that he is in the center of God's plan and God is working out His will through him, that man is invincible. Men and circumstances, whether they mean opposition and threatening or even death, are of no more account than chaff from the threshing floor. Fulfilling the purposes of God is what counts to such a person.

Like Paul, such a man will be obedient to the heavenly vision. He will also believe that no circumstances can exist without God's permission. Paul's attitude was this: "If God wants me to die in this thing, then I am ready to die." This was also Elijah's attitude. Even weak Samson in his last moments before his death, prayed for God's strength that he might serve Him just once more. He recognized that he had played the fool, but he wanted only one more opportunity, and God gave it to him. Samson killed more Philistines then than in all of his previous experience. But it cost him his life to do it.

Elijah had been alone with God. He had been tested and trained and taught. He knew his God and was ready for whatever Ahab might try to do. The monarch's first words were, "Art thou he that troubleth Israel?" I am not sure how Ahab said that, but I have a feeling he was shaking in his boots. He was standing before a man who had been standing in the presence of God. Though Ahab could say to his servants, "You do this and do that," and though he was surrounded by his bodyguard, I am sure he was awed in the presence of Elijah.

The king's accusation was false, and under such circumstances the normal reaction is for a person to justify himself. The Spirit-filled man, on the other hand, has surrendered all his rights and has no self to justify. Elijah might have moderated the king's displeasure by telling him that rain was on the way, but that was not the message Ahab needed at that moment. The king and his people must be brought to judgment and humbleness before God. God's glory was at stake and His honor must be vindicated. That was the first thing to be done. Thus Elijah's answer was fearless. He sought no favor from the king.

Elijah Charges Ahab

Even though Ahab's bodyguard was with him and would have slain Elijah at the king's command, the prophet minced no words. These soldiers held no terror for him. The language in which he spoke is seldom heard in our day in rebuke to leaders of nations who are doing wrong. "I have not troubled Israel; but thou, and thy father's house, in that ye have forsaken the commandments of the Lord, and thou hast followed Baalim."

Men are quick to flatter and to seek their own praise. This

could have happened to Elijah as he stood before Ahab, but it did not. Elijah had been in God's school of training and had been hidden away with God for three and a half years. There Elijah had learned how to stand in the Name of God before men, regardless of who the men might be.

Another tendency is for us to deal in a general way when speaking of human sin. To pick out the sin and name it and denounce the sinner as Elijah did, is quite a different matter. He said to Ahab very much what Nathan said to David: "Thou art the man."

Paul in writing to Timothy gives us further insight into this matter of speaking the truth: "I charge thee therefore before God, and the Lord Jesus Christ, who shall judge the quick and the dead at his appearing and his kingdom; Preach the word; be instant in season, out of season [this facing of Ahab was certainly out of season]; reprove, rebuke, exhort with all longsuffering and doctrine. For the time will come when they will not endure sound doctrine; but after their own lusts shall they heap to themselves teachers, having itching ears; And they shall turn away their ears from the truth, and shall be turned unto fables. But watch thou in all things, endure afflictions, do the work of an evangelist, make full proof of thy ministry" (II Tim. 4:1-5).

Like our Lord himself, we are to speak nothing of ourselves, but that which the Father gives us. As ambassadors for Christ we are to beseech men to be reconciled to God (II Cor. 5:20). We are "vessels" which God fills with His life, His courage, His grace, His power and His strength.

Elijah's charge against Ahab and his house was that they had departed from God and had rejected His Word. Any group or nation that does this ends up in trouble as did Ahab and Israel. People are telling us today that we here at Back to the Bible are old-fashioned. They say times are changing and we have more scientific knowledge, so why should we preach an old gospel from an old Bible? But this is the same spirit that said of Christ: "We will not have this man to rule over us." This was Ahab's attitude. He would not have God to rule over

him nor his house nor his people. This is the attitude of the
so-called liberal in our churches today.

But is it not also the attitude of many of us who would not
by word of lip deny the Lordship of Jesus Christ? We may not
reject His rulership in so many words, but our activity shows
we reject it. Our lack of surrender indicates it. Our failure to
give our life over to Him unreservedly is proof that we are not
having Him rule over us. We do not refuse Him as personal
Saviour, but we refuse Him the place of Lord and Master. We
want the good things of life, but if He touches our lives or
property or finances, or maybe calls our children for His work,
then like the Christ rejectors of old, we say, in effect: "No, we
don't want this man to rule over us."

This story of Elijah and Ahab is history and was written
for our benefit. We must apply it to our own hearts if we are to
be helped by it.

Elijah, as the representative of God, issued orders to Ahab.
The prophet commanded and the king complied. This was an
unusual situation. Here was a man without a government
position. The king looked on him as a mortal enemy. He had
prayed that it should not rain and it did not rain, and because
of that Ahab wanted to arrest and kill him. Yet he had the au-
dacity to say to Ahab, "Send, and gather to me all Israel unto
Mount Carmel, and the prophets of Baal four hundred and fifty,
and the prophets of the groves four hundred, which eat at
Jezebel's table."

God, by signs and wonders and mighty deeds, was going
to overthrow Baal in one day. This is not stated at this point,
but this is what God is leading up to in the directing of these
events. Apostasy has to be judged, and God, who is longsuffering, must eventually bring whatever judgment is needed to
correct the wrong situation.

The world will witness just such a judgment when the
Lord brings down His wrath upon the world church that will
deny the Lord Jesus Christ to be the Eternal God come in the
flesh, and impose its own ideas on men. The picture is drawn
for us in Revelation 17 and 18 where we learn that the world
church will be brought to its end in a very brief space of time.

"Her plagues come in one day, death and mourning, and famine; and she shall be utterly burned with fire: for strong is the Lord God who judgeth her" (Rev. 18:8).

A little later the Scriptures say, "Alas, alas, that great city Babylon, that mighty city! for in one hour is thy judgment come. . . . For in one hour so great riches is come to nought. . . . for in one hour she is made desolate."

In the light of such departure from the living God there is only one thing that believers can do with regard to such a church organization. God's instructions are, "Come out of her, my people, that ye be not partakers of her sins, and that ye receive not of her plagues. For her sins have reached unto heaven, and God hath remembered her iniquities. Reward her even as she rewarded you, and double unto her double according to her works: in the cup which she hath filled fill to her double" (vv. 4-6).

It was because he was a man of faith that Elijah spoke so boldly and courageously to Ahab. We are told in Hebrews 11:34: "Out of weakness were made strong, waxed valiant in fight, turned to flight the armies of the aliens." This is what faith will do. The judgment on the prophets of Baal and their religion was ordained of God; Elijah was the man he had selected to be His representative.

Elijah's weapons were not carnal. They were the same kind of weapons we have for our warfare, weapons mighty through God to the pulling down of strongholds, casting down imaginations and every high thing that exalts itself against the knowledge of God, and bringing into captivity every thought to the obedience of Christ (II Cor. 10:3-5). This is what takes place when faith lays hold of God's promises and acts in obedience.

Ahab dared not disobey. Though he had been raging throughout the country for years seeking Elijah's life, now that he stands before him, he fears. The king saw that Elijah was a man of God and that the power of God was back of him, so Ahab sent for the people of Israel and gathered the prophets of Baal together with them on Mount Carmel.

The king was made a coward by his sins. His conscience

accused him. At a later time in history, Herod, when he heard about Jesus, thought it was John the Baptist come back to life. When Paul stood a prisoner before Felix, it was Felix who trembled. Paul was in chains, but he reached the conscience of the ruler before him. Mary, Queen of Scots, feared John Knox's prayers more than she feared the armies of England. Evil men may put on a false front before the man who is God's messenger, but inwardly they tremble, for the truth of God pierces the heart.

CHAPTER SIX

THE HOUR OF GOD'S TRIUMPH

An altar to Baal had been erected on Mount Carmel. Long before that, however, one had been erected to the Lord, but for many years it had been in ruins. The place chosen was prominent and accessible. It was not some out-of-the-way area hidden from the eyes of men. Such places men look for when they want to hide their sins: "Every one that doeth evil hateth the light, neither cometh to the light, lest his deeds should be reproved" (John 3:20). God chose Carmel to expose the sin of Israel and to demonstrate His own power and glory.

Ahab complied with Elijah's orders to gather Israel and the prophets of Baal at Mount Carmel. He had no other choice, for beggars cannot be choosers. Unless Elijah gave the word there would be no rain. The famine would continue. So, in spite of all of his threats against Elijah's life, Ahab the king was obedient to the prophet's commands and did as was required. This was also a demonstration of the power of God over the hearts of men: "The king's heart is in the hand of the Lord, as the rivers of water: he turneth it whithersoever he will" (Prov. 21:1).

The Psalmist knew that God rules in the hearts and councils of men and said, "Open thy mouth wide, and I will fill it. But my people would not hearken to my voice; and Israel would none of me. So I gave them up unto their own hearts' lust: and they walked in their own counsels. Oh that my people had hearkened unto me . . . I should soon have subdued their enemies, and turned my hand against their adversaries. The haters of the Lord should have submitted themselves unto him" (Ps. 81:10-15).

At a still later time Jehoshaphat recognized the same truth

69

and declared, "God . . . art not thou God in heaven? and rulest not thou over all the kingdoms of the heathen [world]?" (II Chron. 20:6).

God worked not only in Ahab's heart but in the hearts of the Israelites also. He subdued the king so that he obeyed Elijah's orders, and He also made the people of Israel willing to gather together at Mount Carmel. Even the 450 prophets of Baal attended, though the other 400 prophets of the groves may have anticipated what was to follow, for apparently they did not respond to the command to meet at Carmel. It is very possible that all of Israel and the king's household and the false religious leaders who came to Carmel had contempt in their hearts for Elijah; nevertheless, a power beyond themselves caused them to come.

Mount Carmel is located on the northwest corner of Palestine. It rises out of the Mediterranean Sea, the first plateau being about 500 feet above the sea. The peak of the mountain is some 1740 feet above sea level, and a little to the southeast of it is a great plateau about 1680 feet in altitude. Years before the temple was built, an altar had been erected there to the God of Israel, but that had long since been discarded. Prominent in that place in Elijah's time was an altar to Baal. Carmel was known as "the place of the burning."

Northeast of Mount Carmel ran the river Kishon which never went dry. A precipice with a shear drop of about 1400 feet followed the edge of the river, and this was where the prophets of Baal were executed. Some authorities claim that these men were simply pushed over the edge and died on the sharp rocks beneath.

Still farther east was the city of Jezreel. In it Ahab had a second palace in which he lived on special occasions.

There must be a gap in time between verses 20 and 21 of I Kings chapter 18. Verse 20 tells us that Ahab sent word to all the children of Israel and gathered Baal's prophets together at Mount Carmel. This would take time. It was when they were gathered, according to the 21st verse, that "Elijah came unto all the people."

The gathering of this great crowd must have been a

remarkable sight to behold. We can imagine Elijah going to the highest point of the mountain and watching the people as they came by the thousands. The prophets of Baal must have made a colorful picture as they approached in their priestly garments, putting on all the pomp they could to impress the people with their dignity and power. Then would come the king with his noblemen and soldiers. Very likely there were many chariots. There would also be a great chair from which Ahab could watch the proceedings, and around which the dignitaries of his kingdom would stand.

Knowing of Elijah's experience since his prayer of faith that had started the drought, we can be sure that in these days of waiting he spent much time alone with God. He would want to know every detail of God's will with regard to the coming contest. Undoubtedly, he had looked for and found the altar of God that had been thrown down. Then there would be the problem of gathering wood and locating water. There were several such places, but nearby was one that never ran dry even in the dryest of seasons. He would also find out from God where the execution of the false priests was to take place so that when the test was made on Carmel there would be no hitch in the proceedings.

All eyes were upon Elijah as he came to the people. Ahab looked at him in anger and fear, the priests in contempt, the people divided in loyalty but expectant and awed by what they saw. Though Obadiah is not mentioned he would be looking on from somewhere near the king's retinue.

Elijah was God's man standing against the nation of Israel, its king and leaders and its false priests, but he showed no fear. He took complete control and said, "How long halt ye between two opinions? if the Lord [Jehovah] be God, follow him: but if Baal, then follow him. And the people answered him not a word" (I Kings 18:21).

Though he was a man of like passions as we are, Elijah met this situation by faith in God and not by any inherent power in himself. Without a question God's legions of angels surrounded him as he confronted this wicked king and his subjects. By faith the prophet subdued a kingdom, worked righteousness and escaped the edge of the sword. This is what the man whose faith is in God can do. This is what Elijah did and what we also can do when the time and the situation require it.

Elijah's Challenge to Israel

Seven times during the course of that great memorial day, Elijah spoke and his words were the true index of his heart. His first words were addressed to the people of Israel, not to the prophets of Baal when he asked, "How long halt ye between two opinions?"

Ahab and his subjects had all been trained in the knowledge of the true God. Most of them, however, including Ahab, had turned to the false worship of Baal. Others again were undecided. The word "halt" means "totter." The vast majority of them were tottering between following Baal or following Jehovah. No doubt they dreaded the Lord because they had seen the result of the great famine in their land. Yet these same people wanted to curry the favor of the king because they were his subjects; and in order to do so they tolerated the religion of Baal.

Elijah demanded a definite decision on their part. There was only one true God, the God of Abraham, of Isaac and of Jacob, the great "I am." Beside Him there was no other God. He will not accept a divided heart on the part of His people.

We, too, have our decision to make in this day. We must decide between the god of materialism and the God of grace. We cannot serve God and mammon. The individual who is not for Christ is against him. A person who does not gather with Christ scatters abroad. Joshua had to put this issue clearly to the people of Israel in his day. He said, "And if it seem evil unto you to serve the Lord, choose you this day whom ye will serve . . ." (Josh. 24:15). Years ago Edmund Burke, a British statesman said, "All that is required for evil to conquer is for good men to do nothing."

An indictment against the Laodicean church was this: "I know thy works, that thou art neither cold nor hot: I would that thou wert cold or hot. So then because thou art lukewarm, and neither cold nor hot, I will spue thee out of my mouth"

(Rev. 3:15,16). It was the Lord himself who said this. Neutrality with regard to spiritual things is not possible.

James tells us, "A double minded man is unstable in all his ways" (1:8). Jonathan, the son of Saul, was a man who loved David. He knew God's plans for David and was well aware that he would one day sit upon the throne of Israel. Nevertheless, Jonathan chose to stay with his father instead of joining David and his fellow outcasts. God did not allow Jonathan to live to see David raised to the throne. The young prince died on the battlefield with his father.

Among the religious leaders of our Lord's day were those who believed on Him: "But because of the Pharisees they did not confess him, lest they should be put out of the synagogue: For they loved the praise of men more than the praise of God" (John 12:42,43). How much better had they followed the principle that was later stated in Hebrews 13:13: "Let us go forth therefore unto him without the camp, bearing his reproach."

Perhaps some who read this are halting between two opinions concerning salvation. Perhaps they think salvation is in the church and that by joining the church or following its rules and regulations all will be well with them. But why not listen to God instead? True salvation lies only in the Lord Jesus Christ, made possible through His shed blood. The Lord himself clearly stated what the decision must be when He said, "Except a man be born again, he cannot see the kingdom of God" (John 3:3).

Will we, like the people of Israel, not answer a word when challenged? Theirs was the great sin of indecision already referred to in connection with the Laodiceans. They were not making a choice and yet the Lord's word to them was, "I stand at the door, and knock: if any man hear my voice, and open the door, I will come in to him, and will sup with him" (Rev. 3:20). Indecision is actually unbelief. There is no neutral ground with regard to Christ. When Elijah challenged his fellow countrymen, they answered him not a word. They feared Ahab and the priests of Baal and were not ready to commit themselves.

God was calling on His ancient people to repent just as He did the church in Ephesus in Revelation and as He is doing today. The Lord said to that early church: "Nevertheless I have somewhat against thee, because thou hast left thy first love. Remember therefore from whence thou art fallen, and repent, and do the first works; or else I will come unto thee quickly, and will remove thy candlestick out of his place, except thou repent" (2:4,5). We must make a decision.

To the church of Pergamos the Lord stated: "So hast thou also them that hold the doctrine of the Nicolaitanes, which thing I hate. Repent; or else I will come unto thee quickly, and will fight against them with the sword of my mouth" (2:15,16). These warnings are not to be lightly turned aside. It is God who speaks to our hearts and to our consciences. Let us answer Him with willing and obedient hearts.

Having thrown out that challenge, Elijah continued, "I, even I only, remain a prophet of the Lord; but Baal's prophets are four hundred and fifty. Let them therefore give us two bullocks; and let them choose one bullock for themselves, and cut it in pieces, and lay it on wood, and put no fire under: and I will dress the other bullock, and lay it on wood, and put no fire under: And call ye on the name of your gods, and I will call on the name of the Lord [Jehovah]: and the God that answereth by fire, let him be God. And all the people answered and said, It is well spoken" (I Kings 18:22-24).

In saying that he was alone, Elijah did not mean that God was not with him. What he meant was that there was no other prophet to help him. The prophets of Baal were many and he gave them first opportunity to see if their god would answer by fire.

From another standpoint they could not complain because Baal was the sun god and the god of fire. The worship of Molech was also the worship of Baal. In several places in the Bible we read of the people of Israel passing their children through the fire to Molech. Seeing the reasonableness of Elijah's proposal, the people assented to it at once, and this forced the prophets of Baal out into the open. They were put in the position of complying with the challenge or acknowledging that Baal was an imposter.

Yet the challenge went beyond that. It was an acid test of

Elijah's faith. He gave the challenge but could not produce the result; God himself had to provide that. The question in many minds must have been, "Will God answer?" They did not have to wait long to find out.

Sowing and Reaping

According to Galatians 6:7 a man reaps whatever he sows. If he sows to the flesh he will reap corruption, but if he sows to the Holy Spirit, he will of the Holy Spirit reap life everlasting. God, you see, will not be mocked. Elijah was sowing to the Spirit and could not fail to reap of the Spirit. The prophet knew what God's answer would be.

He stood alone of all the prophets of God, for though there were 7000 persons in Israel who had not bowed their knee to Baal, they had largely gone "underground" and were hiding perhaps in caves or in the mountains and had no public ministry.

It was very possible that some of these persons were in the group that stood on Mount Carmel, but if they were, they did not make their presence known. Elijah stood alone—yet not alone for God was with him. Someone has said that one man with God is a majority. This certainly proved out on Mount Carmel.

In this connection Revelation 3:8 has encouraged me again and again. Our Lord said to the church at Philadelphia: "I know thy works: behold, I have set before thee an open door, and no man can shut it: for thou hast a little strength, and hast kept my word, and hast not denied my name." The group was small, but it honored God and God blessed them for it.

Numerically the forces of unrighteousness in the world are in the majority. This was true at Mount Carmel, but the greatest power did not rest with them. Baal had his followers by the thousands and apparently they were united. In fact, we have a common saying to the effect that in union there is strength. But we must qualify that. It all depends on the kind of union. If a man is united with God in performing a work that God has determined shall be done, then even one man with God on his side can successfully stand against the whole world. A union composed of large numbers of people can well prove to be a weak giant because a man-made union is based on unrighteousness.

This is one reason why God isolates His servants. It is then they realize that their strength lies in Him and not with the large number of followers who might have been attracted to their banner. Elijah with God could and did stand against the whole kingdom of Israel even though Ahab was there with a show of force, and the prophets of Baal were there in large numbers.

God constantly seeks for a man to do His work. He said through Ezekiel: "I sought for a man among them, that should make up the hedge, and stand in the gap before me for the land, that I should not destroy it: but I found none" (22:30). For this reason God had to give His sinning people over to judgment.

At an earlier time in their history, God did find such a man when the nation of Israel rebelled against Him. Psalm 106:23 gives us the information: "Therefore he said that he would have destroyed them [Israel], had not Moses his chosen stood before him in the breach, to turn away his wrath, lest he should destroy them." Here is a case where one man standing in the gap saved a whole nation.

Elijah was such a man in his day. He had intimate fellowship with God and by knowing his God he did exploits. Such a man cannot be deflected from his goal no matter what the circumstances are in his life. At a crisis time in his experience Job said, "Though he [God] slay me, yet will I trust in him" (13:15). A little later the same patriarch said, "For I know that my redeemer liveth, and that he shall stand at the latter day upon the earth: And though after my skin worms destroy this body, yet in my flesh shall I see God: Whom I shall see for myself, and mine eyes shall behold, and not another; though my reins be consumed within me" (19:25-27). Job knew of God's intimate watch care over him and that He had knowledge of his every thought. This believer of old said, "He knoweth the way that I take: when he hath tried me, I shall come forth as gold" (23:10). No wonder Job came through his trying experiences in triumph.

Because David knew God he was not afraid to face Goliath. The whole army of Israel fled in terror before the giant but not the son of Jesse. He said to the Philistine: "Thou comest to me with a sword, and with a spear, and with a shield, but I come to thee in the name of the Lord of hosts, the God of the armies of Israel, whom thou hast defied. This day will the Lord deliver thee into mine hand; and I will smite thee, and take thine head from thee; and I will give the carcases of the host of the Philistines this day unto the fowls of the air, and to the wild beasts of the earth; and all the earth may know that there is a God in Israel. And all this assembly shall know the Lord saveth not with the sword and spear: for the battle is the Lord's and he will give you into our hands" (I Sam. 17:45-47). What faith this was!

Many Christians today shrug off these episodes of history and say that these were all right for the Old Testament believers, but they are not for us today. God still has a work that He wants done and He will give the grace and the strength and the power needed to accomplish it. "What shall we then say to these things? If [since] God be for us, who can be against us? He that spared not his own Son, but delivered him up for us all, how shall he not with him also freely give us all things?" (Rom. 8:31,32). What more assurance do we need than this?

The god too many Christians think of is too small to be the God of the Bible. We bring shame on ourselves and on our God by our lack of faith. Paul said, "I can do all things through Christ which strengtheneth me" (Phil. 4:13). And again in II Corinthians 9:8 Paul declared: "God is able to make all grace abound toward you; that ye, always having all sufficiency in all things, may abound to every good work."

Ahab and all Israel knew that God had withheld rain from their land for three and one-half years. What is more, the prophets of Baal had been able to do nothing about it. Undoubtedly, they had tried but were unsuccessful.

The next test was to be a test by fire. This was within the supposed realm of the followers of Baal, for he was considered to be the lord of the sun. His devotees were consecrated by passing through the fire. Consequently, if any god could answer by fire, surely Baal could. His prophets could not refuse this challenge without admitting they were imposters.

Fire is something that God has used on many occasions. There is little doubt that when Cain and Abel brought their offerings before the Lord, God showed His acceptance of Abel's offering by sending fire to consume it (Gen. 4:4,5).

When Abraham wanted to know how he stood with God, the Lord told him to bring an offering, and then sent fire to burn it up (Gen. 15:17).

God said He would judge Sodom and Gomorrah and the cities of the plains. This He did by sending fire to destroy them (Gen. 19:24).

God revealed Himself to Moses by means of the burning bush in the desert. Here again, God spoke through fire (Ex. 3:2).

In leading the people of Israel out of Egypt through the desert and into the land of Canaan, God used a cloud by day and a pillar of fire by night (Ex. 13:21). When at the beginning of their journey they came to Mount Sinai and God gave them the law, He spoke to them through thunder and lightning and an earthquake and a fire (Ex. 19:18).

As a means of accrediting the tabernacle worship and its offerings, God sent fire from heaven to consume the burnt offering on the brazen altar. Leviticus 9:24 says, "And there came a fire out from before the Lord, and consumed upon the altar the burnt-offering and the fat: which when all the people saw, they shouted, and fell on their faces." In this case God was showing approval, but in the following chapter in Leviticus we have the record of two sons of Aaron who brought strange fire before the Lord, "And there went out fire from the Lord, and devoured them" (Lev. 10:2).

When Solomon had finished the building of the temple and the first offerings were prepared on the altar, God showed His approval by sending fire (II Chron. 7:1).

So it was that in Elijah's day God was going to employ fire to accredit His work and His servant. He would later send water, but what Israel needed was first the fire of judgment to show that the sacrifice which was a substitute for their national sins was accepted before God.

Summary of Fire in the Bible

We can summarize the Bible teaching concerning fire in the following way. First of all, fire is a symbol of the presence of God. This we saw when God appeared to Moses in the burning bush.

Fire is also an indication of God's acceptance of a sacrifice. On a number of occasions in the Old Testament, God showed that He was pleased with certain sacrifices by sending fire from heaven to consume them.

In the New Testament the work of the Holy Spirit is symbolized under the figure of cloven tongues as of fire (Acts 2:3).

Fire will be used also with regard to God's judgment on unbelievers at Christ's Second Coming. Take such a passage for example as II Thessalonians 1:8,9: "In flaming fire taking vengeance on them that know not God, and that obey not the gospel of our Lord Jesus Christ: Who shall be punished with everlasting destruction from the presence of the Lord, and from the glory of his power."

Peter also tells us that God will judge sinners and sin with fire saying, "The day of the Lord will come as a thief in the night; in which the heavens shall pass away with a great noise, and the elements shall melt with fervent heat, the earth also and the works that are therein shall be burned up" (II Pet. 3:10).

In the last book of the Bible the awful destiny of the lost is also connected with fire: "And death and hell were cast into the lake of fire. This is the second death. And whosoever was not found written in the book of life was cast into the lake of fire" (Rev. 20:14,15).

Finally, fire is connected with God's judgment of the believer's works. We learn from the Scripture, "Every man's work shall be made manifest: for the day shall declare it, because it shall be revealed by fire; and the fire shall try every man's work of what sort it is. If any man's work abide which he hath built thereupon, he shall receive a reward. If any man's work shall be burned, he shall suffer loss: but he himself shall be saved; yet so as by fire" (I Cor. 3:13-15). It is a dangerous matter to play with fire especially God's fire. All who play with sin or count sin as a light thing, are playing with fire.

Purpose of Fire on Mount Carmel

As has been pointed out before, the fire Elijah called for was to fall upon the slain bullock laid upon the altar. The slain animal symbolized the substitute for the sins of the people of Israel. If no substitute came between the people and their sins, they would have to bear the fire of God's wrath themselves. But an acceptable substitute would exhaust God's wrath and the people would go free. Sin had to be judged either in the person of the sinner or in a substitute. Only Elijah's God, however, could send such fire.

For God to answer by fire was also to be an evidence of the efficacy of prayer.

In the third place the fire was to make clear who was the true God – Elijah's God or Baal.

Elijah had appealed to the conscience of the people when he asked them how long they would totter between two opinions. They answered him nothing on that one. Then he spoke to their reason when he suggested that the two bullocks be slain and placed one on each altar and the God who answered by fire would be the true God. When it was a matter of conscience the people were quiet. But when it was a matter of seeing the wonders of God through a method that appealed to their reason, they gave their approval. They came in great numbers to see this, but so far as their heart condition was concerned, most of them stayed cold and hard. They looked to see a miracle, but they were deaf to God's call to repentance.

The prophets of Baal chose a bullock and dressed it, but as Elijah had warned, they put no fire under it. "They took the bullock which was given them, and they dressed it, and they called on the name of Baal from morning even until noon, saying, O Baal, hear us. But there was no voice, nor any that answered. And they leaped upon the altar which was made. And it came to pass at noon, that Elijah mocked them, and said,

Cry aloud: for he is a god [that is Baal is a god to his prophets]; either he is talking, or he is pursuing, or he is in a journey, or peradventure he sleepeth, and must be awaked. And they cried aloud, and cut themselves after their manner with knives and lancets, till the blood gushed out upon them. And it came to pass, when midday was past, and they prophesied until the time of the offering of the evening sacrifice, that there was neither voice, nor any to answer, nor any that regarded" (I Kings 18:25-29).

As the majority group they had been given first chance. Because there were so many of them it took them but a very short time to prepare the sacrifice. As is often the case in matters that pertain to God, however, the majority was on the wrong side.

When Elijah admonished these idolatrous priests not to put any fire under their offering, he was warning them that he would not stand for any tricks. This they had often resorted to and deceived people; what they were now doing was out in the open with many eyes watching them. There was no opportunity given to these tricksters and imposters to insert fire in any way into Baal's altar.

It is a sobering thing to realize that at the judgment of the Great White Throne there will be no opportunity for tricks or deceit on the part of those charged with sin and rejection of Christ. Everything will be in the open. The Scripture passage will be completely fulfilled which says, "Be sure, your sin will find you out."

It was not beyond the power of Satan to have sent fire and to have thus deceived the people with regard to Baal and his prophets. With God's permission the Evil One was allowed to send fire which burned up Job's sheep and servants (Job 1:16). According to Revelation 13 the beast out of the earth will make the inhabitants of the earth worship the Antichrist and will do great wonders, one of which will be to make fire come down from heaven (v. 13). But in this open trial between Satan and God on Mount Carmel no fire fell through the power of the false priests. There is no false religion that can put away sin by sending fire to consume the vicarious sacrifice. No false religion can bestow the Holy Spirit. The prophets of Baal were doomed to failure.

Baal's Frenzied Priests

Dr. Edersheim in his Bible history gives the following account of this scene based on authentic information: "Now commenced a scene which baffles description. Ancient writers have left us accounts of the great Baal-festivals and they closely agree with the narrative of the Bible, only furnishing further details. First rose a comparatively moderate, though already wild, cry to Baal; followed by a dance around the altar, beginning with a swinging motion to and fro. The howl then became louder and louder, and the dance more frantic. They swirled round and round, ran wildly through each other's ranks, always keeping up a circular motion, the head low bent, so that their long dishevelled hair swept the ground.

"Ordinarily the madness now became infectious, and the onlookers joined in the frenzied dance. But Elijah knew how to prevent this. It was noon — and for hours they had kept up their wild rites. With cutting taunts and bitter irony Elijah now reminded them that, since Baal was Elohim, the fault must lie with them. He might be otherwise engaged, and they must cry louder.

"Stung to madness, they became more frantic than before, and what we know as the second and third acts in these feasts ensued, the wild howl passed into piercing demoniacal yells. In their madness the priests bit their arms and cut themselves with the two-edged swords which they carried and with lances. The blood began to flow, the frenzy reached its highest pitch, when first one, then others, commenced to prophesy, moaned and groaned, then burst into rhapsodic cries, accusing themselves, or speaking to Baal, or uttering incoherent broken sentences. All the while they beat themselves with heavy scourges, loaded or armed with sharp points, and cut themselves with swords and lances — sometimes even mutilated themselves — since the blood of the priests was supposed to be specially propitiatory with Baal."

The frenzy of Baal's prophets reached its height when the

sun was at its highest point at noon. In the excitement generated by the rhythm and speed of the priests' action, it would not have taken a great deal for the people watching them to have been swept off their feet emotionally and to have joined in the wild orgy. But Elijah was ready for this very thing. He very effectively used the weapon of sarcasm to expose the pretentions of these evil men and at the same time to insure emotional stability among the watchers.

We read in Psalm 2:4 how God will laugh and hold in derision the plots of men who rebel against His government. It was something like this that happened when Elijah spoke as he did. God was using a human instrument and a human life but with supernatural power back of it. These men were fools and God was answering them according to their folly.

God shows His mind again on this matter in Proverbs 1: "Because I have called, and ye refused; I have stretched out my hand, and no man regarded; But ye have set at nought all my counsel, and would none of my reproof: I also will laugh at your calamity; I will mock when your fear cometh; When your fear cometh as desolation, and your destruction cometh as a whirlwind; when distress and anguish cometh upon you. Then shall they call upon me, but I will not answer; they shall seek me early, but they shall not find me: For that they hated knowledge, and did not choose the fear of the Lord: They would none of my counsel: they despised all my reproof. Therefore shall they eat of the fruit of their own way, and be filled with their own devices" (vv. 24-31).

It is possible that Israel had never seen such earnestness and enthusiasm at any previous time. But such things are no proof that the cause is good and true. Some people assume that such a display of zeal and fervor is evidence of spirituality; however, this can be far from the truth.

Elijah Prepares the Sacrifice

Another three hours passed and it was time to call off the futile efforts of the idolatrous priests.

Elijah called the people of Israel to come near to him and he repaired the altar that had been broken down. This was the time of the evening sacrifice and final preparations were now made for God to answer by fire.

The people were invited to come close, because he wanted them to witness every move. Elijah wanted them to see that there was no trickery in what he was doing. Truth does not fear the closest investigation. It does not shun the light; in fact, it courts it. The altar so long broken was a silent witness of the broken fellowship of the people with their God. It first had to be repaired. Before God could remove the judgment of the drought, their sin must be taken care of.

The principle on which God was working appears in II Chronicles 7:12-15: "And the Lord appeared to Solomon by night, and said unto him, I have heard thy prayer, and have chosen this place to myself for an house of sacrifice. If I shut up heaven that there be no rain, or if I command the locust to devour the land, or if I send pestilence among my people; If my people, which are called by my name, shall humble themselves, and pray, and seek my face, and turn from their wicked ways; then will I hear from heaven, and will forgive their sin, and will heal their land. Now mine eyes shall be open, and mine ears attent unto the prayer that is made in this place."

Israel's broken altar should remind us of the danger of our altars being broken down. What is our relationship with God? Is it something that is kept intact daily? Or is there a lack of repentance in our hearts? God's instruction to Israel in the passages quoted from II Chronicles is also His recipe for a revival in a Christian's heart.

Before any of us can do anything for the Lord we must be in right relationship with Him. Then we must seek to arouse our fellow Christians to do the same thing. After succeeding here we can reach out for lost souls. Unfortunately, many of us turn these things around. We preach concerning the lost but overlook the need of our own relationship and fellowship with God. We must first get right with Him before we can do an adequate job of pointing others to Him. And if there is sin in the life which we have not confessed and do not repent of, we block our own approach to God. "He that covereth his sins shall not prosper: but whoso confesseth and forsaketh them shall have mercy" (Prov. 28:13). Or as the Psalmist said, "If I regard iniquity in my heart, the Lord will not hear me" (Ps. 66:18).

The Lord had to remind the church at Ephesus that they had left their first love, and unless they returned He would have to remove the candlestick out of its place. When Abraham went down to Egypt during a lapse of faith, it was only after he came back to the altar that he had a new beginning and fresh promises from God.

It is very significant that though Elijah was dealing with the Northern Kingdom during the time of the division of Israel, he took twelve stones thus signifying Israel's oneness and unity. So far as God's will for them was concerned, they were not to be a divided people.

Once the altar was set up Elijah had a trench dug around it and water poured on the sacrifice and the wood until the trench was full.

The Altar

There are lessons to be learned from the significance of this whole arrangement concerning the altar. The altar itself speaks of prayer and surrender. The trench which was dug around the altar stands for complete separation from any man-made rituals. God's truth has its source in God and not in men. The woman at the well asked our Lord where worship should be conducted, in Jerusalem in the temple, or on the mountain set apart by the Samaritans for that purpose. Our Lord told her that the time was coming when the true worshippers of God would worship Him in Spirit and in truth without the need of any special place designated for it. True worship is not something created by man. We gather together in our churches and the services should be conducive to worship. But though there may be an emotional atmosphere present that makes people think they are worshipping, it may not be true worship at all.

Wood was laid on the altar and was necessary for the burning of the sacrifice. The wood speaks of the cross and points forward to the crucifixion of our Lord. Finally, there is the sacrifice itself on which the fire was to fall. For the fire to fall was not enough; it must fall on the proper object. Fellowship between God and His people could be restored only as the proper sacrifice was accepted by Him through fire.

We could never get into right relationship with God had there not been Christ's substitutionary death for us on Calvary. He was the sacrifice offered on our behalf. It is only through Him that we can approach God. Had He not died, we would be aliens from God today.

The part the water played in this sacrifice was unique. The fact that it was poured over the bullock and the wood and filled the whole trench until the entire altar was soaked with water and surrounded by water, insured that no ordinary power would be able to consume the sacrifice. It almost appeared that Elijah was making it hard for God to answer. But there is nothing too hard for God. It is possible that this water was obtained at a spring that never ran dry, located close to the place of sacrifice. It has been suggested, however, that these people who had come at Elijah's command may have brought their own skins of water. It was a very precious commodity at that time since it was so scarce. They may have been induced to bring their water and pour it on the altar. If they did, their action would speak to us of laying things that we hold precious on the altar of sacrifice.

God calls on us to present to Him the most precious thing that we have. Paul tells us about this in Romans 12:1: "I beseech you therefore, brethren, by the mercies of God, that ye present your bodies a living sacrifice, holy, acceptable unto God, which is your reasonable service."

Some may think that their body is not the most precious thing in the world to them, but Satan was right with regard to the average heart when he asked God for permission to afflict Job and said, "Skin for skin, yea, all that a man hath will he give for his life. But put forth thine hand now and touch his bone and his flesh, and he will curse thee to thy face." The Lord gave Satan permission to afflict Job's body but did not permit him to take Job's life. The record in Job is that Satan went forth "from the presence of the Lord, and smote Job with sore boils from the sole of his foot unto his crown." Job did not react as Satan predicted but it was not because the patriarch undervalued his body.

Most of us will do anything we can to keep our bodies in the condition we would like to have them. We will spend all of our savings if need be to keep them healthy or to keep them alive as long as possible. The body is precious indeed and that is what God wants us to bring to the altar. Of course, in yielding the body we yield also ourselves. God wants the whole person.

Elijah told the people to pour water on the altar not once but three times. They obeyed and the whole sacrifice and altar overflowed with water. This reminds us that we may come before God and claim to have surrendered all, but the Lord may tell us to go and check everything again. When God does so it is well for us to ask Him to check our lives and then we will be surprised what He will find. As we go to the Word, the Spirit works in our hearts and searches us to the depths of our beings. This we will have to do over and over again. God accepts us as far as we have gone, but as we go deeper into the Word, He reaches deeper into our hearts. He wants everything laid on the altar.

As surrendered and devoted to the Lord's cause as was the Apostle Paul he had to admit to the Philippian believers that he had not yet attained. In order to apprehend that for which he was apprehended he said he was going to forget those things which were behind and reach forward to the things which were before (Phil. 3:12,13).

As we seek the face of God, and the only way we can seek His face is to have Him shine the light of His word upon us, He will show us the evil in our hearts. When we turn from the evil revealed to us, God will hear us as we pray (II Chron. 7:14).

Elijah's Prayer

By having water poured over the sacrifice as often as he did, Elijah closed all doors to any human counterfeits or trickery. Then he began to pray: "And it came to pass at the time of the offering of the evening sacrifice, that Elijah the prophet came near, and said, Lord God of Abraham, Isaac, and of Israel, let it be known this day that thou art God in Israel, and that I am thy servant, and that I have done all these things at thy word. Here me, O Lord, hear me, that these people may know that thou art the Lord God, and thou hast turned thy heart back again" (I Kings 18:36,37).

This is a short prayer of 63 English words (even less in the Hebrew), and it takes some 20 seconds to speak them. But the prophets of Baal had prayed to their idol for six solid hours and received no answer at all. Elijah prayed for 20 seconds and God answered by fire.

We will find great value to analyze this prayer of Elijah. He addressed it to the unchangeable God, the God of Abraham, Isaac and Jacob or Israel, the latter name meaning "A Prince with God." This God is one who never changes. He is our God.

Elijah did not have some special influence with God. The prophet was a man of like passions as we are. When he addressed God, however, he sought the vindication of God's name. He said, "Let it be known this day that thou art God in Israel." Here was no selfish prayer for self-aggrandizement. Elijah sought only the honor of God.

It was then that Elijah asked God that He would make it plain to the people that he, Elijah, was God's servant. A servant, as Elijah used this word, speaks of one who is entirely surrendered to another. Christian service, for example, is not really something that we do for Christ. It is doing the things He has assigned us to do, not what we decide we will do. Furthermore, we do not do those things, it is Christ who lives in us. It is through total commitment to Him that His work is accomplished in each believer.

Elijah was a servant like that. He was willing to be hidden from public gaze. He was willing to be fed mysteriously for three and a half years, willing to face the man who wanted badly to take his life, willing to stand in the lowest place, or at the highest place as he did on Mount Carmel if only God might be honored.

On the surface, at least, the prophets of Baal did not lack devotion to their God. Yet in spite of all their earnestness and their pleading and their frenzy they received no answer. The reason is that they were worshippers of the sun and the sun is not a god. The sun is the creation of the God whom Elijah worshipped, the unchangeable God of Abraham, Isaac and Jacob, the God and Father of our Lord Jesus Christ.

The earnestness of Elijah's prayer differed in character from that of the prophets of Baal. The Lord describes it through James when He says, "The effectual fervent prayer of a righteous man availeth much" (5:16).

Some, even in Christian circles, seem to misunderstand what is meant here. They shout in prayer as though God were deaf. They put on a demonstration as though they had to attract God's attention. Earnestness in prayer is not physical gesticulation but a condition of the heart and will with regard to the purposes of God.

Perhaps here we may learn to examine our own prayers. Since Elijah's prayer was motivated by his desire to see God honored, God answered His servant. In writing concerning prayer James said, "Ye ask, and receive not, because ye ask amiss, that ye may consume it upon your lusts" (4:3). Right motive is an essential for answers to prayer.

The Fire Falls

It is only as we ask according to the will of God that God hears us (I John 5:14). Elijah was on Mount Carmel in the will of God and his prayer pleased the Lord. He cried, "O Lord, hear me, that this people may know that thou art the Lord God, and that thou hast turned their heart back again" (I Kings 18:37). It was then that the fire of the Lord fell and consumed the burnt offering and the wood and the stone and the dust and licked up the water that was in the trench (v. 38). There was no long wait for this answer. The prophets of Baal had prayed for six hours with no results. Elijah spoke this brief prayer and God answered.

God's long-suffering and mercy had already been in evidence. For years He had put up with Israel's backsliding. God is not willing that any should perish but that all should come to repentance, but He will not hold His anger against sin forever. Since He is a righteous God He must judge, but He knows the right time to do it.

Elijah had called to the people to come near where he was standing by the altar and they obeyed. Then the fire fell and consumed all that was on and around the altar but none of the people were touched. The fire descended in the presence of all, but directly on the altar, not on the people.

This was no ordinary fire but one exhibiting the wrath of Almighty God. It was supernatural fire that descended from God. It was not the result of spontaneous combustion or of man's work. It did not come as a result of natural law.

It first consumed the offering of the sacrifice. Pictured for us in this is the death of the substitute for man's sin. God in His righteous wrath could have consumed the people but He consumed the sacrifice instead. This reminds us that while we were yet sinners Christ died for us.

A fire usually starts at the bottom and works up but in this case the fire started at the top and worked down. The offering was consumed in point of time before the wood that was intended to burn the offering. This was God demonstrating His wrath against sin and at the same time His love for sinners.

The very stones of that altar were consumed by the fire. Even the dust and the water in the trench were licked up by the flames. There was nothing that could resist this fire from God.

So it will be when God's final judgment falls on those who have rejected the mercy provided through Christ's death. There will be nothing to stop that judgment when it comes. It will be a flaming fire taking vengeance on them that know not God and who obey not the gospel of Jesus Christ. He will punish them with everlasting destruction when He returns to this earth the second time (II Thess. 1:7-9).

In Revelation 20 we are given a fuller view of the judgment of the Great White Throne. All the evidence is before the Divine Judge and those accused: "And whosoever was not found written in the book of life was cast into the lake of fire" (v. 15). This is what our Saviour warned of during the time of

His public ministry when He told of the place where "their worm dieth not, and the fire is not quenched" (Mark 9:44,48).

Elijah acted in faith when he prayed as he did. He had God's Word on which to base his prayer. That is what made it a prayer of faith. He asked God that the answer would be given in such a way that the people would know he was God's prophet, acting on God's Word. God could not refuse such faith so the fire fell.

This scene at Carmel also reminds us of the statement in the Book of Hebrews that says, "Our God is a consuming fire." God is a God of love but He is also a God of righteousness. He cannot overlook sin. Fools mock at sin but God cannot be mocked. If this fire had not fallen on the sacrifice prepared by Elijah, then it would have fallen upon those who had rebelled against Him. A man reaps what he sows, for God is not mocked. At the present God is dealing in mercy and showing long-suffering. There is a day coming, however, when He will be a consuming fire. A man's day of mercy is while he is upon this earth now, not afterwards. That day ends when he passes from this life into the next.

It is to our benefit to remember as believers that the fire of God in our lives consumes the dross of sin and self. Like a refiner of silver, God applies the heat only until the metal is clear (Zech. 13:9; Mal. 3:3).

It is no wonder that the people of Israel at Mount Carmel fell on their faces when the fire fell and said, "The Lord is God, the Lord is God." The great controversy between Baal and God was now ended. Three and a half years of waiting for the drought to end was now over. The people had witnessed the graphic evidence of the power of Jehovah who called Himself "The Great I Am, the Self-Existent One." They bowed before their God and Creator.

JUDGMENT AND MERCY

Baal's Prophets Slain

With God having answered Elijah's prayer by fire and the people showing at least a surface repentance, only one more step was necessary before God could send rain. This had to do with the removal of the prophets of Baal from Israel. They had been holding the people in spiritual bondage and were a constant threat to the future development of God's people. The step which was taken was no cruel act of savagery on the part of Elijah and those who aided him, but like the action of a people defending themselves from alien invasion. Israel belongs to God and the presence among them of priests and prophets of a false religion was an invasion of God's territory.

This has its lessons for us with regard to God's attitude toward sin in our personal lives. We learn in Romans 8:13: "For if ye live after the flesh, ye shall die: but if ye through the Spirit do mortify [make to die] the deeds of the body, ye shall live." God's way of defeating the power of the flesh in the life is to have us put to death the deeds of the body actuated by the fallen nature.

Paul wrote to the Galatians: "They that are Christ's have crucified the flesh with the affections and lusts" (5:24). The same truth is given in Colossians: "For ye are dead, and your life is hid with Christ in God. . . . Mortify therefore your members which are upon the earth; fornication, uncleanness, inordinate affection, evil concupiscence, and covetousness, which is idolatry: For which things' sake the wrath of God cometh on the children of disobedience: In the which ye also walked some time, when ye lived in them. But now . . . put off all these;

93

anger, wrath, malice, blasphemy, filthy communication out of your mouth. Lie not one to another, seeing that ye have put off the old man with his deeds" (3:3-9).

Lying or false communication or what other name we may wish to give it is a serious evil in God's eye. And when it enters into the realm of the spiritual it can be dangerous in the extreme. Back in the Old Testament God warned Israel how they were to deal with prophets who would lead them astray from the truth. The directions are found in Deuteronomy 13:1-5: "If there arise among you a prophet, or a dreamer of dreams, and giveth thee a sign or a wonder, And the sign or the wonder come to pass, whereof he spake unto thee, saying, Let us go after other gods, which thou hast not known, and let us serve them; Thou shalt not hearken unto the words of that prophet, or that dreamer of dreams: for the Lord your God proveth you, to know whether ye love the Lord your God with all your heart and with all your soul. Ye shall walk after the Lord your God, and fear him, and keep his commandments, and obey his voice, and ye shall serve him, and cleave unto him. And that prophet, or that dreamer of dreams, shall be put to death; because he hath spoken to turn you away from the Lord your God, which brought you out of the land of Egypt, and redeemed you out of the house of bondage, to thrust thee out of the way which the Lord thy God commanded thee to walk in. So shalt thou put the evil away from the midst of thee."

To have allowed the prophets of Baal to continue living and exercising all their evil practices would have exposed the Israelites to further corruption. It would have left the impression in the minds of these priests as well as the Israelites that the prophets of Baal though agents of apostasy were immune from judgment. God's Word was that they were all to be destroyed. Not one of them was to escape.

There are some today who would charge God with being cruel for giving such instructions. We are living in an era that has rejected the Word of God and that is absolutely ignorant of His Word and His character. Most people do not know the God of Elijah. They have a philosophy of coexistence with sin and advocate noninterference with sinners no matter what they do.

We as Christians are held responsible by God to put to death in our own lives the instruments of sin. We are not to destroy people but the impulses and desires in our own hearts that would lead us astray. God gives us the weapons by which this can be done, weapons which are not carnal "but mighty through God to the pulling down of strong holds" (II Cor. 10:4,5). This cannot be done through the human will but has to be done in the power of the Spirit.

We learn in Galatians 5:17: "For the flesh lusteth against the Spirit, and the Spirit against the flesh: and these are contrary the one to the other: so that ye cannot do the things that ye would." We must be unsparing in judgment of the evil tendencies and ways in our own lives if we are to let God control us and lead us into a closer walk with Himself. Just as none of the prophets of Baal were to be allowed to escape, so we are not to look with favor on one single sin.

In Joshua 10 we have the account of a great battle fought by Joshua against five kings of Canaan. These were defeated and hid themselves in caves. Joshua's soldiers put rocks in front of the cave so that these men could not escape, and then carried word to their leader. His answer to them was to bring out the kings and not leave them as prisoners; they were to be put to death.

Again, in Deuteronomy 17:2-5, God shows how severe Israel had to be in order to keep false teaching and evil men and women out of the land. "If there be found among you, within any of thy gates which the Lord thy God giveth thee, man or woman, that hath wrought wickedness in the sight of the Lord thy God, in transgressing his covenant, And hath gone and served other gods, and worshipped them, either the sun, or moon, or any of the host of heaven, which I have not commanded; And it be told thee, and thou hast heard of it, and enquired diligently, and behold, it be true, and the thing certain, that such abomination is wrought in Israel: Then shalt thou bring forth that man or that woman, which have committed that wicked thing, unto thy gates, even that man or that woman, and shalt stone them with stones, till they die."

Whereas these were literal and physical facts in Israel's history, the spiritual lesson for us is that sin must be made inactive in our lives. The New Testament teaches us that through identification with Christ we have already died to sin (Rom. 6:1-7). So then it is for us to put into practice by faith in our daily lives what we have in reality under grace in salvation (Rom. 6:11-13).

The people of Israel obeyed Elijah and took the prophets of Baal down the steep mountainside and cast them over the 1400 foot precipice to the rock-infested river below. Soon the waters would rise when the rains came and the bodies of these false prophets would be washed out to sea which was only a short distance away. This was an awful end for these men, but it signals God's hatred for idolatry and for His determination to purge His own people.

What is seen in Israel is often pictured in our own hearts and lives as believers. We have idols at times, because anything that takes the place of God in our lives is an idol. If God is not first – if it is money or our homes or things, these are idols.

Ahab was a witness to all this and may even have assented to it under the enthusiasm of the emotional impression left by the falling of the fire. But if this was the case, it was only temporary, for he was an apostate who after receiving the knowledge of the truth willfully and deliberately sinned (Heb. 10:26-29).

It was not long before Elijah put him again to the test and his real nature showed up. Said the prophet to the monarch: "Get thee up, eat and drink; for there is a sound of abundance of rain. So Ahab went up to eat and to drink" (I Kings 18:41,42).

This is a testimony to the faith of Elijah but it also shows once more the kind of man that Ahab was.

Before Elijah met him and instructed him concerning Mount Carmel, Ahab had been searching for pasture for his mules. Apparently he had little thought for his people. Hundreds of Baal's prophets who had been fed by him and Jezebel had lost their lives, but Ahab was going back to his palace to feast himself. There was no thought of drawing near to God and humbling himself under His mighty hand.

While Elijah went up the mountain to pray, Ahab went to eat, careless of the fact that his land was still suffering even though rain was promised, and that it would continue to suffer as long as a false religion was condoned and promoted by Ahab and his household.

The prophets of Baal had been judged, but Ahab had been allowed to go free. His time was coming. God is a merciful God but He does not hold back His judgment against sin forever.

Elijah Prays for Rain

When Elijah declared that there was the sound of abundance of rain, no rain had as yet fallen. There were no clouds in the sky, no thunder and lightning, nothing that gave visible proof that rain was imminent. There was not a physical sign anywhere that rain was on the way. Elijah's statement was based on his faith or trust in the Word of God.

Elijah knew that the Lord was the Creator and rain was possible only as He allowed it. Undoubtedly, the prophet had read Job 28:26 which says, "When he made a decree for the rain, and a way for the lightning of the thunder." In other words, God said when it would rain, how much it should rain, or how little. He controlled it the same as he also controls the sea into which the rivers run: "When he gave to the sea his decree, that the waters should not pass his commandment: when he appointed the foundations of the earth" (Prov. 8:29). It is the Lord "Who covereth the heaven with clouds, who prepareth rain for the earth, and maketh grass to grow upon the mountains" (Ps. 147:8).

God sent judgment on the world in Noah's time through rain (Gen. 7:4). Through Amos the prophet, the Lord tells us, "And also I have withholden the rain from you, when there were yet three months to the harvest: and I caused it to rain upon one city, and caused it not to rain upon another city: one piece was rained upon, and the piece whereupon it rained not withered" (4:7). This was why though Elijah was a man of like nature or passions as we are, he prayed earnestly that it might not rain and it did not rain for a period of three years and six months. Then he prayed again and the heaven gave rain and the earth brought forth her fruit (James 5:17,18).

It is very likely that only Elijah of all those present heard the sound of the coming rain. It was a sound that only faith could hear, and Ahab had no faith. Elijah demonstrated the truth of Hebrews 11:1: "Faith is the substance of things hoped for, the evidence of things not seen." God told Elijah it was going to rain and Elijah believed Him and acted upon what God had said. That is faith.

Elijah went to the top of Carmel and cast himself upon the earth and put his face between his knees. He did not hang around to receive the congratulations of the people on the successful outcome of his contest with the prophets of Baal. He needed once more to be alone with God. While Ahab went to feast, Elijah had food, like our Saviour, that men knew nothing of.

It is well for us who preach the gospel to follow each preached sermon with supplication for further manifestation of God's grace and power. Perhaps one reason why more is not accomplished through our preaching today is that we do not take time to pray after we have preached.

Elijah stood as a giant among the people at the contest on Mount Carmel. When he went higher on the mountain and came into the presence of God he came as a poor sinner who needed mercy, and he humbled himself. In facing the forces of Baal, he was as bold as a lion. When he was alone with God, he hid his face and declared himself to be of no worth.

Elijah had his servant with him when he went to the top of Carmel to pray, and after he had made intercession he "said to his servant: Go up now, look toward the sea. And he went up, and looked, and said, There is nothing. And he said, Go again." Seven times they went through this, and at the seventh time the servant said to his master: "Behold, there ariseth a little cloud out of the sea, like a man's hand. And he [Elijah] said, Go up, say unto Ahab, Prepare thy chariot, and get thee down, that the rain stop thee not. And it came to pass in the mean while, that the heaven was black with clouds and wind, and there was a great rain. And Ahab rode, and went to Jezreel."

Separation

There are eight different aspects of this prayer that we should consider. First of all Elijah withdrew himself from the crowds. He had boldness to enter into the holy place, but this was only because of the blood-bought way provided by Another. It called for humility on his part. The prophet did not stand before God proud and arrogant. He did not seem to express a great deal of happiness for what had happened on Carmel. He put his face between his knees as he spoke to God.

The Bible tells us to have "boldness to enter into the holiest." How is this done? The same passage tells us it is done by the blood of Another. We do not enter into God's presence brashly, or with swagger or boasting. We do as our Lord told us to: "But thou, when thou prayest, enter into thy closet, and when thou hast shut thy door, pray to thy Father which is in secret; and thy Father which seeth in secret shall reward thee openly" (Matt. 6:6).

Elijah shut himself off from everybody else so that he could be shut in with the Lord. This is one of the hardest lessons to learn in prayer, that of shutting out the world and being alone with the Lord. By this we do not mean simply the physical separation into a private place, but the calming of the human spirit which is so easily upset by the turmoil of the day. "Be still and know that I am God," the Lord has said. The atmosphere of the world is fatal to the spirit of devotion so it must be left behind when we enter into God's presence. We must take time to rest before Him. We do not rush into His presence and start praying and speak for five minutes and then end our prayers. Real praying takes time.

Humility

In the second place Elijah's posture shows he was humble and reverent before God. Before the crowds he was majestic and dignified. As God's ambassador he pleaded with Israel.

But as Israel's intercessor he pleaded with Almighty God in humility of heart and spirit.

The great victory he had just won did not cause Elijah to take liberties with God. He did not approach the Lord with indecent familiarity but as a humble supplient before His God. In Hebrews 4:16 we are told to come boldly to the throne of grace that we may obtain mercy and find grace to help in the time of need. But this does not mean that we come as God's equal. It does mean that we come with confidence, knowing that when we come in the name of Christ, the Father will hear us.

Peter instructs us in these words: "Humble yourselves therefore under the mighty hand of God, that he may exalt you in due time: Casting all your care upon him; for he careth for you" (I Peter 5:6,7). James also makes reference to this when he says, "But he giveth more grace. Wherefore he saith, God resisteth the proud, but giveth grace unto the humble. Submit yourselves therefore to God. Resist the devil, and he will flee from you" (4:6-8). Before Moses could come close to the burning bush he had to take off his shoes, because he was standing on holy ground.

Those who face sin in the firmest manner, bow the lowest before Almighty God. John who wrote the Gospel bearing his name and three short letters and also the Book of Revelation was one who leaned on the breast of Christ, but he took no liberties with his Lord. When he was taken up by the Spirit into heaven and given a view of his glorified Lord, he said, "I fell at his feet as dead" (Rev. 1:17).

Confidence in God's Word

In the third place Elijah based his prayer upon the promises of God. God had told him to go and show himself to Ahab, for He would send rain upon the earth. Was it necessary with such a promise for this man to beg God to fulfill what he said he would do? The promises are given, not to restrain prayer, but to encourage prayer. God gives us promises to show the direction in which we should pray and to what extent we may expect an answer. These promises are the signed checks which we must endorse and present for payment. Our Lord himself, while living on this earth, asked of the Father through prayer. It was to Him that the Father said in Psalm 2: "Ask of me, and I shall give thee the heathen for thine inheritance." The inheritance is assured to the Son, but He is told that He must ask for it. The promise is given, then it must be claimed, first by prayer and then by faith. This is the message of Matthew 7:7,8: "Ask, and it shall be given you; seek, and ye shall find; knock, and it shall be opened unto you." James reminds us that sometimes we have not because we ask not. Prayer, then, is saying, "Amen" (so be it) to God's promises.

Definite

In the fourth place Elijah's prayer was definite. He did not generalize. He was specific in what he requested. Too often we simply say "God bless" this one or that one but we ask for nothing in particular for them.

Some time back I received a letter from a man who wrote concerning many interesting things and at the close asked me to answer him. The matters he wrote about, however, were of such a general nature that I did not know what he wanted, so I wrote to him asking what it was that he wanted to know.

He sent the second letter just as general as the first. It left me no further ahead than I had been before. This is often the way we approach God with regard to requests for different individuals or organizations. Let us be specific in our asking. We have been blessed with all spiritual blessings in heavenly places in Christ. This is a definite promise and assurance from the Word, so let us, on this basis, ask God for special and particular things in our prayers.

Fervent

In the fifth place Elijah's prayer was fervent. He prayed earnestly. We do not need to shout and scream in order to show God that we are in earnest. This is a mistake some people make. They shout as if they had to shake the walls of heaven before God could hear them.

An angel wrestled all night with Jacob, and when the Lord

finally wanted to leave, His servant Jacob prayed earnestly. He said, "I will not allow you to leave me unless you bless me." He had a very definite thing in mind. He was deeply in earnest. It was then that God could do specific things for him.

Concerning our Saviour himself we read in the Book of Hebrews: "Who in the days of his flesh, when he offered up prayers and supplications with strong crying and tears unto him that was able to save him from death, and was heard in that he feared" (5:7). This was definite, fervent praying on the part of our Lord.

Watchfulness

The sixth aspect is that Elijah prayed with watchfulness. When he asked God for rain, then he sent his servant to look to see what was happening in the sky. The first time the servant came back and reported there was nothing, so Elijah sent him again, but the lad brought back the same report. The Bible instructs us to watch and pray, not to wonder and pray. Elijah had an expectant faith and believed God would answer. Mark 11:24 says, "Therefore I say unto you, What things soever ye desire, when ye pray, believe that ye receive them, and ye shall have them."

Perseverance

In the seventh place we find that Elijah prayed with perseverance. He prayed and then sent his servant to look. This occurred again and again. Six times the answer came back that there was nothing to be seen. It is when we wait patiently for the Lord that He inclines unto us and hears our cry (Ps. 40:1). God will not break His Word. He is a God of truth, but we must wait for His time. None of us who wait upon the Lord shall be ashamed. He grants the answer but sometimes He waits to lead us to a point of real intensity in perseverance.

Assurance

The eighth characteristic of this prayer of Elijah's was the assurance of an abundant answer. "And it came to pass at the seventh time, that he said, Behold, there ariseth a little cloud out of the sea, like a man's hand. And he said, Go up, say unto Ahab, Prepare thy chariot, and get thee down, that the rain stop thee not." Then it was that the heavens became black with clouds whipped by a great wind, and the rain fell. In the meantime Ahab rode toward Jezreel.

While Elijah had been living at the home of the widow of Zarephath, a handful of meal had been all that they had seen at any time; yet it had been enough to sustain the household for many months. Consequently, a cloud the size of a man's hand was all that was needed for Elijah to know that his prayer was answered. This was why God had led him step by step through the various experiences and trials for the last three and a half years.

How we need to learn to trust God! He prepares us day by day for greater things that are coming. "All things work together for good" we read in Romans 8:28, but do we believe it?

Ahab was urged to journey swiftly to his destination for soon the river Kishon would be overflowing and he had to cross it while he had the chance.

The little cloud the size of a man's hand was the first fruit of the tremendous clouds that were to cover the sky and pour out their waters. Between that first small cloud the servant saw and the time when the heavens were completely overcast was sufficient time for Elijah's servant to get word to Ahab. A long time before Elijah had told Ahab that it would not rain except he, God's prophet, said so. Now he was telling Ahab that it would rain. This, of course, was all based on the Word of God. God speaks truth. He cannot lie.

Not only did Ahab ride toward Jezreel but Elijah girded up his loins and ran before him to the entrance to the city. The rain poured down and, without a doubt, most of the people who appeared at Carmel were soon thoroughly drenched. In light of the drought conditions that had existed for so long, they would all be thankful in spite of the fact that they were thoroughly soaked.

The scene as depicted in I Kings is remarkable. There was Ahab surrounded by his nobles, riding in all his pomp to Jezreel eighteen miles away. Then the rain began to fall and ahead of the king ran Elijah, the prophet, in the power of the Lord. The countryside that had seen so much sun and so little rain was one moment dry and hot with scant grass and trees showing the ravages of the drought. Then the sky was suddenly filled with dark clouds, the lightning flashed, the thunder rolled, and the rain poured down. The hand of the Lord was upon His prophet and Elijah outran the chariot eighteen miles to the gates of the city.

Elijah girded himself for this race which reminds us of the frequent lessons in the New Testament concerning the race we run and the need of being properly girded for it. We are told to "lay aside every weight, and the sin which doth so easily beset us, and let us run with patience the race that is set before us, Looking unto Jesus the author and finisher of our faith" (Heb. 12:1). We have a race to run, so let us run it prepared in God's way for it.

CHAPTER EIGHT

A MIGHTY MAN FALLS

The events on Mount Carmel had provided a day of triumph for God's servant. Following the miracle of the fire that fell and consumed the offering was the ending of the drought in answer to Elijah's prayer. As Ahab raced toward Jezreel in the pouring rain, Elijah girded up his loins "and ran before Ahab to the entrance" of the city. After one of the hardest days in any man's experience, Elijah, under the power of the Lord, outran the king's chariot for 18 miles.

It was shortly after this that a reaction set in. Ahab went home and told Jezebel all that had transpired on Mount Carmel including how Elijah had slain all the prophets of Baal with the sword. The infuriated queen then sent a message to the prophet in which she said, "So let the gods do to me, and more also, if I make not thy life as the life of one of them by tomorrow about this time" (I Kings 19:2).

The man who just a short time before ran before Ahab's chariot to the glory of the Lord, now ran for his life. "And when he saw that, he arose, and went for his life, and came to Beersheba, which belongeth to Judah, and left his servant there. But he himself went a day's journey into the wilderness, and came and sat down under a juniper tree: and he requested for himself that he might die; and said, It is enough; now, O Lord, take away my life; for I am not better than my fathers" (I Kings 19:3,4).

Elijah had been in the thick of a spiritual warfare against forces seen and unseen. The Satanic powers had been ranged against him, but with strength provided by the Lord he had fought and won a great victory over them. The armor of God was upon him as he engaged in the battle and emerged triumphantly. Then, shortly after, he suffered a spiritual downfall. The question is, how could such a thing take place and how can we who are persons of like nature to Elijah escape such a fall?

Spiritual warfare must be begun and carried on in humility. Paul's words come to us with new force as we read: "Finally, my brethren, be strong in the Lord, and in the power of his might. . . . For we wrestle not against flesh and blood, but against principalities, against powers, against the rulers of the darkness of this world, against spiritual wickedness in high places" (Eph. 6:10-12). This Elijah knew and he wore the whole armor of God in the battle.

When he girded himself to run to the city of Jezreel, he took a humble place before King Ahab. He assumed a servant's place as one who wanted to honor his king. Though Elijah rebuked this monarch for his idolatry, he still honored him for the office he held.

Our Saviour's ministry was conducted in humility. We read in Philippians 2: "Let this mind be in you, which was also in Christ Jesus: Who, being in the form of God, thought it not robbery to be equal with God: But made himself of no reputation" (vv. 5-7). Just prior to His death our Lord showed this humble spirit when He washed the disciples' feet. This was a lesson to them and to all who call him Saviour and Lord that they are to live and serve not in pride but in humility.

Something of Ahab's character is seen in that he let Elijah run before the chariot. This man of God who had brought such a triumph that day should have been invited to sit with the king as he journeyed on toward his home in Jezreel. In fact, Elijah should have been raised to the place of Prime Minister, but Ahab cared nothing for the glory of God even after the terrible lesson he had witnessed on Mount Carmel.

There can be no question but that Elijah was hoping for an all-out revival in Israel. It may have been hope of this that helped give him the extra strength to continue to run those many miles. He wanted to see what would happen when news of these events came to Jezebel who was, in reality, the cause of idolatry in Israel. Perhaps she would break before God as the people had when they cried out, "The Lord he is God; the Lord he is God."

On the surface, at least, Ahab seemed to have broken before God. He had consented to the death of Baal's prophet. He sat back and did not raise a hand in protest as these wicked men were brought to judgment. He seemed to assent to all the things that took place on Mount Carmel so that Elijah must have felt there was the possibility of a real and deep revival. No doubt the prophet hoped the day would end with Jezebel coming to terms, realizing that she could not trifle with the things of God.

Elijah went no farther than the gate of the city but Ahab went on to his palace and told Jezebel all that Elijah had done.

It is very possible that it was with a great degree of enthusiasm he told his wife of the fire that fell from heaven and consumed the offering and the wood and the stones and even the dust and the water. After her own prophets had labored for six hours and nothing had happened, Elijah had prayed a brief prayer and God had immediately answered. This was a miracle, indeed, and caused the people to shout to the glory of God. Then he would tell her about the slaughter of the prophets of Baal. Perhaps there was a secret hope in his heart that she, too, would be convinced that she must honor God. He undoubtedly was convinced, but he was not regenerated. He knew what he ought to do, but he himself had no change of heart.

This is often the case with people. They become convinced of the truth of the gospel but they do not follow it through to the place where they accept Christ as personal Saviour. Nicodemus was such a person for he was convinced that the Lord Jesus could only do the things that he was doing because God was with Him. But our Lord told this Jewish leader that he needed to be born again. We cannot get away from that truth: "Except a man be born again, he cannot see the kingdom of God" (John 3:3).

There was a fatal omission in Ahab's narration of events. He told her all that Elijah had done, but not what the Lord had done. The difference is simply this. Ahab was a man who was convinced that Elijah was a prophet of God, but he himself not having been born from above, could not see that the happenings on Mount Carmel were the Lord's doing. Ahab praised a man. He told how all the people were for Elijah. He showed how the authority of the priests of Baal evaporated. Elijah said that he had prayed that it would not rain, and it did not rain for three and a half years. He had also said that it would not rain until he asked God to make it rain, and this had taken place just as he said it. In spite of this wealth of evidence she was not convinced.

Jezebel's Threat

Perhaps Ahab was amazed at her reactions. It takes no stretch of the imagination to visualize her face becoming red with anger as she listened to the recital of the death of her prophets. Ahab was a weakling whom Jezebel easily stirred up to do what she wanted. In modern terms we would describe him as a hen-pecked husband who did very much what his wife told him to. Jezebel's vicious and vindictive character showed up in the message she sent to Elijah: "So let the gods do to me, and more also, if I make not thy life the life of one of them by tomorrow about this time."

She was crafty and unscrupulous and merciless. Ahab was a weak tool in her hands. She was the foreshadowing of the religious woman spoken of in Revelation, chapter two. There she is used as a symbol of an evil seducer leading God's people astray: "Notwithstanding, I have a few things against thee, because thou sufferest that woman Jezebel, which calleth herself a prophetess, to teach and to seduce my servants to commit fornication, and to eat things sacrificed unto idols. And I gave her space to repent of her fornication; and she repented not. Behold, I will cast her into a bed, and them that commit adultery with her into great tribulation, except they repent of their deeds" (vv. 20-22).

The Lord was addressing a church in apostolic days, but He was also speaking to much of the organized church of today which is no longer teaching the truth of God but the false doctrines of Jezebel.

Then in Revelation 17:3, we find the consummation of this

system in the woman who sits upon a scarlet colored beast, the woman who is Mystery, Babylon the Great, the Mother of Harlots and Abominations of the Earth.

Jezebel was a woman insensible to the presence of divine power, but her tongue was set on fire of hell. James says, "And the tongue is a fire, a world of iniquity: so is the tongue among our members, that it defileth the whole body, and setteth on fire the course of nature; and it is set on fire of hell" (James 3:6). She knew she could not harm the Lord, but she sought to take her revenge on God's chosen servant. Let us not forget that those who live godly in Christ Jesus shall suffer persecution.

Jezebel's Fear

Jezebel knew that God was almighty, and in spite of the fact that she threatened God's servant, she was afraid of him. She had the authority to send soldiers to take his life that very moment, but her announcement was such that he had 24 hours to flee. Actually she did not dare lay a hand upon him. Apparently she hoped that what she had threatened would be sufficient to make him leave the country.

It is not unusual for people to put on a bold front with regard to spiritual things. It is only a front however, for back of it is a heart of fear. Many are afraid to face the issues of life and eternity and act as though they had resolved all of these matters and had no further concern with them.

Some years ago I conducted an evangelistic campaign in a church that did not want public invitations to be given. I announced, however, that anyone who wanted to talk to me about the Lord Jesus Christ and salvation should stay after the meeting. At one of those after meetings among those remaining to speak to me was a young man whom I knew. I asked him, calling him by name, "Would you like to be saved?"

He answered, "No."

I then asked him why he was staying for the after meeting. He answered: "I am afraid to go to hell."

He did not want to be saved, but he was afraid of hell. I finally said to him, "I will be praying that God will make you willing to be saved."

At 12 o'clock that night he came to see me. By that time he wanted to be saved.

Let us not lie to ourselves and others concerning our spiritual fears. There is no point in trying to hide them from God, for He sees our hearts. Let us turn to Him through faith in Christ and find the solution to our spiritual perplexities.

Elijah's reaction to Jezebel's threat was not consistent with his character as we have seen it in these studies. We would have looked for him to lay hold in confidence on God. The promise in Isaiah is, "Thou wilt keep him in perfect peace, whose mind is stayed on thee: because he trusteth in thee. Trust ye in the Lord for ever: for in the Lord Jehovah is everlasting strength" (26:3,4). But there was no peace of mind or heart with Elijah. He ran for his life.

Previous to this when he was confronted with danger, the word of God came to him very clearly. When Elijah's life was in danger for having told Ahab that it could not rain until he said so, God warned him to hide himself. When the brook dried up, he was instructed to go to Zarephath. Then, after three and a half years had passed, Elijah was instructed to show himself to Ahab because God was going to send rain. These orders were all clear and definite. But no word came to him from God concerning this threat. The prophet left on his own account.

Had he not sought orders from God? Perhaps he did, but there is nothing in the record that says he did. Elijah could not see behind the scenes, so he did not know what was going on in Jezebel's heart. He did not stop to think that if she had meant to kill him, she could have done so right then and there, when she sent the messengers with the warning. Evidently there was a lesson that this good man needed to learn. He was a spiritual giant who had stood up for God but his success could have led to his destruction. Apparently God temporarily withdrew His hand from Elijah's life and let him think for himself for a little while.

It was after Paul had been caught up into the third heaven and received wonderful revelations from God that he received a thorn in the flesh. God allowed this to come lest elation and pride, because of the great revelations given him, would lead him astray (II Cor. 12:7-9).

Here was Elijah who had successfully consummated one of the greatest feats in history. It is true that God did it through him, but Elijah was the instrument, and there was the grave danger that he might become proud. This is a danger that always confronts men who are successful servants of the Lord. This is where Satan has caught many of them unawares and has succeeded in causing their withdrawal from effective service. The principle involved is illustrated well in the case of Saul, Israel's first king. Samuel, speaking for the Lord said, "When thou wast little in thine own sight, wast thou not made the head of the tribes of Israel, and the Lord anointed thee king over Israel? And the Lord sent thee on this journey, and said, Go and utterly destroy the sinners the Amalekites, and fight against them until they be consumed" (I Sam. 15:17,18).

Saul went against the Amalekites but he did not obey God with reference to their complete destruction. So he was rejected for his pride and rebellion.

Three Possible Reasons

There were possibly three major reasons why the Lord temporarily allowed Elijah to follow his own devices. The hand of the Lord had been upon Elijah all that day, even to the outrunning of Ahab's chariot. Now, God did not desert him, but temporarily withdrew Himself, first of all for Elijah's own sake. He did not want His servant to become a prey to Satan and be useless to God. Elijah needed to see that within himself he could not do the work of God. Pride is a subtle thing and unless it is checked it can end our usefulness.

The second reason was possibly that God intended to discipline Israel because they had not returned to Him with their whole heart. They had to reap the fruit of their own sowing. It is possible that if Elijah had stayed with them, his presence might have stood in the way of their just punishment.

In the third place, God possibly wanted to take Elijah to a solitary place where He could speak to him alone and reveal Himself to him in a fresh way. He could have done this by a specific command, but apparently Elijah reached a decision before God's mind was made plain to him, and this is why he ran.

Elijah was not forsaken. His experience reminds us that whom the Lord loves He chastens and that if we are not chastened we are not sons (Heb. 12:6-10). Regardless of how chastening comes, it is not at the moment a joyous experience but a grievous one. Afterwards it yields the peaceable fruit of righteousness to those who are exercised by it.

Elijah first came to Beer-sheba which was in Judah and left his servant there. This was outside of Ahab's kingdom. The prophet continued a day's journey into the wilderness and sitting down under a juniper tree asked God to let him die.

God dealt gently with His servant and sent an angel to awaken him and have him arise and eat. Elijah was refreshed and strengthened and lay down and slept once more. The second time the angel came to him and said, "Arise and cat; because the journey is too great for thee" (I Kings 19:7).

Elijah must have realized then that he had depended upon his own intellect and discernment. He was a man of such faith that he had seen and heard the rain before it ever fell. Yet he was only human, after all, a man of like passions as we are. Through the Psalmist the Lord promises, "I will instruct thee and teach thee in the way which thou shalt go: I will guide thee with mine eye" (32:8). We need to depend on God's wisdom not our own.

It was by trusting in what he thought looked good to him that led to Lot's downfall. "And Lot lifted up his eyes, and beheld all the plain of Jordan, that it was well watered every where, before the Lord destroyed Sodom and Gomorrah, even as the garden of the Lord, like the land of Egypt, as thou comest unto Zoar. Then Lot chose him all the plain of Jordan; and Lot journeyed east; and they separated themselves the one from the other" (Gen. 13:10,11). There were several downward steps that Lot took according to the record in this chapter, and each one of them was the result of leaning on his own wisdom.

The case of the twelve spies who were sent into the land is another illustration of men looking at things according to their own viewpoint and not seeing these things as God sees them. The account is given in Numbers 13. There we learn that ten of the spies came back with this report: "And there we saw the giants, the sons of Anak, which come of the giants: and we were in our own sight as grasshoppers, and so we were in their sight" (v. 33). Their decision was reached on the basis of what they saw and not what God wanted them to see.

When a person looks at things as God sees them, he chooses a way of life in line with God's desires. We read of Moses that by faith he forsook Egypt "not fearing the wrath of the king: for he endured, as seeing him who is invisible" (Heb. 11:27). Faith gave Moses vision that went beyond what the human eye can see. This was the happy experience of Job at the end of his trials, for he said, "I have heard of thee by the hearing of the ear: but now mine eye seeth thee" (42:5,6).

Job had a new vision of the Lord; he understood why things were as they were; and he abhorred himself and repented in dust and ashes.

Elijah, when he received the threat from Jezebel, looked at it with the eyes of human reason and ran for his life. This time he did not run for the Lord. One translator puts it, "He went whither he would." There was uncertainty to his steps this time. He had no divine direction, no word from God as to where he should go. Let us always be careful to know that we are following in the path that God has laid out for us.

Some would tell us that a need constitutes a call. But if that were the case, some of us would have to be 100 persons, instead of one. In our own work here at the Broadcast we receive hundreds of letters from people telling us of a great need. These needs are all around us, but we must know from God what particular need it is that we are to meet. In this way our steps are sure and the work is certain to be that which God wants us to do. Otherwise, we would be working in circles and the work of God would not be done.

The following song, by Mary Slade, pictures for us the blessings that follow us when we closely follow the Lord.

Footprints of Jesus

Sweetly, Lord, have we heard Thee calling,
Come follow me!

And we see where Thy footprints falling
  Lead us to Thee.

Tho' they lead o'er the cold, dark mountains,
  Seeking His sheep;
Or along by Siloam's fountains,
  Helping the weak;

If they lead through the temple holy,
  Preaching the Word;
Or in homes of the poor and lowly,
  Serving the Lord.

By and by, through the shining portals,
  Turning our feet,
We shall walk with the glad immortals,
  Heav'n's golden street.

Footprints of Jesus
  That make the pathway glow;
We will follow the steps of Jesus,
  Where'er they go.

Not Forsaken

Those servants of God who show that they have great zeal and courage for God and His truth when left to themselves become weak and timid. This may explain why there is so much weakness and timidity in Christian work today. Do we not know that all things are possible with God, and that without Him nothing is possible?

We can praise God that He does not forsake His people. He is faithful to us and watches over us though He gives no visible manifestations of His presence. Israel did not enter the promised land when she should have, yet God did not forsake her though He temporarily removed His hand of blessing. He assured them: "Be strong and of a good courage, fear not, nor be afraid of them: for the Lord thy God, he it is that doth go with thee; he will not fail thee, nor forsake thee" (Deut. 31:6).

When Moses was about to depart he called Joshua to him and said in the presence of all Israel: "Be strong and of good courage: for thou must go with this people unto the land which the Lord hath sworn unto their fathers to give them; and thou shalt cause them to inherit it" (Deut. 31:7). God's promise to us is: "I will never leave thee, nor forsake thee" (Heb. 13:5). The Patriarch Job suffered the loss of his family, his wealth and his health, yet he was never forsaken of God.

Our Lord is the only One serving God who was ever forsaken. He cried out while on the cross: "My God, my God, why hast thou forsaken me?" He was forsaken in order that we who turn to God through faith in Him would never be forsaken.

We forget it but God never does that "we have this treasure [the presence of God] in earthen vessels, that the excellency of the power may be of God, and not of us" (II Cor. 4:7). This is why He tells us that He has chosen that which the world calls foolish and weak and base. It is through such that He glorifies His own Name. This is why Paul reminds us that none of us in our work for the Lord is anything; only God counts, for He gives the increase. The words are, "So then neither is he that planteth any thing, neither he that watereth; but God that giveth the increase" (I Cor. 3:7).

Someone has said, "The best of men are but men at their best." This God wants us to know: let God's power be withdrawn, even for a moment, and one sees that men are but earthen vessels absolutely valueless and useless in themselves. This is why the Psalmist says, "Verily every man at his best state is altogether vanity" (39:5). Man left to himself is a failure as Ecclesiastes 7:20 fully recognizes: "For there is not a just man upon earth, that doeth good, and sinneth not."

Noah left to himself got drunk. Lot left to himself became carnal. Abraham, at a time he did not depend on God, lied concerning his wife. Moses forgot for a moment where his strength lay and became angry. Aaron failed to remember that it was God who had assigned different responsibilities to his servants so became jealous. Joshua left to himself became careless and hasty in his decision with regard to Ai and also the Gibeonites. David grew careless as to the source of his strength and committed adultery and murder. Peter became self-sufficient and denied his Lord. These things happen to us as soon as we, even for a short while, leave God out of our lives.

It was in order to give us lasting examples and instruction that God had recorded for us the experiences of these men of old and of Israel. Paul tells us this in I Corinthians 10:11-13: "Now all these things happened unto them [Israel as a nation and individuals in the nation] for ensamples: and they are written for our admonition, upon whom the ends of the world are come. Wherefore let him that thinketh he standeth take heed lest he fall. There hath no temptation taken you but such as is common to man: but God is faithful, who will not suffer you to be tempted above that ye are able; but will with the temptation also make a way to escape, that ye may be able to bear it." Because others fail we need not fail. God has given us these examples from their lives so that we might be forewarned and forearmed, trusting ourselves to His keeping and distrusting our own strength.

Still, we find it very easy to criticize another servant of God. When he falls or falters we tend to find fault with him. What we often forget is that the testings others face may be far greater than what we ourselves have to cope with. It is our responsibility to pray for fellow believers and uphold them before the Lord.

The exercise of faith must be a constant thing as we walk with God. We do not exercise faith in this aspect of salvation once for all. For the new birth we trust Christ once for all and are born into His family. Then there is no condemnation to them who are in Christ Jesus. It is only after we are born again that we can walk with God, but this must be done in the power of the Spirit and in the exercise of the life of Christ within us.

Romans 8:4 says that God will fulfil His will in us who walk not after the flesh but after the Spirit. It is a walk, a daily walk, a step at a time. It is a life of faith lived moment by moment. Faith itself is a divine gift from God and comes through the Word of God. Faith comes by hearing and hearing by the Word of God, according to Romans. So Galatians 2:20 is appropriate again in this respect: "I am crucified with Christ: nevertheless I live; yet not I, but Christ liveth in me:

and the life which I now live in the flesh I live by the faith of the Son of God, who loved me, and gave himself for me."

We must, then, be sympathetic with Elijah, for after all he was but a man. He wanted to give up just as we sometimes are tempted to give up. God, however, never gives up. The Lord wants His own character to be seen in us, and He will make this possible if we will but lean upon Him. Paul wrote to the Corinthians: "Therefore, my beloved brethren, be ye stedfast, unmoveable, always abounding in the work of the Lord, forasmuch as ye know that your labour is not in vain in the Lord" (I Cor. 15:58).

I have met servants of God who have allowed circumstances and circumstances alone to direct their path. At such times I have felt that what they were doing was not in the will of God for them, but what could I say? Sometimes they approached me apologetically and sought to justify what they were doing, declaring that they were having good opportunity to witness for the Lord. Yet they knew and I knew that such was not the case. My heart was heavy for them.

Elijah's Depression of Soul

Elijah traveled on foot some eighty-five miles to the southern border of Judah. Then he took another day's journey into the wilderness, and by that time he was completely exhausted. He was a man of remarkable physical strength and endurance, but he had extended himself to the breaking point. There was first of all the preparation for the "showdown" with the prophets of Baal at Mount Carmel. There was great nervous pressure upon him because of Satanic opposition while he was on the mountain. Then came the time when it was necessary to slay 450 prophets of Baal. Such invasion of Satan's territory is not done easily. Then Elijah prayed for rain with great earnestness; and finally he ran 18 miles to Jezreel to see what results would follow the great triumph at Mount Carmel. All of this took place in one day. Satan knows that a tired body is an added opportunity for him, and he took advantage of it in this case. When Jezebel's threat was delivered to Elijah, he seemed to lose control and continued running until the time we find him under the juniper tree.

It was then he requested that he might die. He felt his labors had been fruitless. His soul longed for rest. "It is enough," he said. He had hoped to see a great revival but no spiritual change had taken place in Israel.

I must admit that there are times when I have wondered after 26 years of preaching on the radio with millions of people listening in our country and in other lands, just what is the end of this work. God has called us to faithfulness, however, not to success. My hope and trust lies in Him. Is this how we trust Him for the work He has given us to do?

Some men in the Bible went even further than Elijah did in discouragement. Jeremiah said, "Cursed be the day in which I was born." Job wished that the day of his birth might perish. These all were men of like passions as we are. They showed what they could be when God filled them and controlled them, and what they were when left to themselves. If we were not given this knowledge of them we would be tempted to think they were super-human beings instead of ordinary mortals like the rest of us.

How inconsistent we can be when we are not walking with the Lord. When Elijah fled from Jezebel, he "fled for his life" the Scripture says. When we find him under the juniper tree he pleads: "Lord take my life." Life, however, is a precious commodity to each of us, and Elijah was no exception. The picture was not all bad with regard to this man of God for in his dejection he turned to the Lord. Though he was still depressed he unburdened his heart before God.

How often when things have gone wrong have we turned away from the Lord in dejection and depression. Sometimes we have even accused Him of mistreating us. But there is no such thing here with Elijah. He was on talking terms with the Lord, though God did not answer his request for death. He had asked amiss; he was not praying in the Spirit. In fact Elijah never died, for God took him to heaven without passing through the portals of death.

God knew that His servant had overtaxed himself and needed a renewal of his physical life as well as his spiritual life. Our inner life is very sensitive to our outward condition. Rest is very important to all of us. Proper exercise is also important. These things we sometimes forget but God does not. Our physical condition can reflect upon our spiritual condition.

Elijah felt very much alone. This is what he said to God: "I am left alone." Loneliness sometimes is a penalty that men pay for being great men. Our Lord was the most lonely person who ever walked this earth. Someone sent me the following paragraph:

"A leader is a lonely man. He follows visions that others cannot see. He moves ahead when others lag behind. He walks in solitude with God. Driven on by burning desire to achieve goals that to others seem visionary or impractical (because leaders are not conformists), they are looked upon with suspicion by the run-of-the-mill crowd. Men who lead are certain targets for the biting barbs of criticism. Their fearless, clear compelling manner make them a prey to those who do not understand them. But the church needs leaders today – men who will bear criticism, who will bear reproach for the cause of Christ; men who will stand up when others fall, who will go on when others faint. Will you be a leader?"

God does not leave such men, however, without help. The following poem is a testimony to the faithfulness of the women who have stood back of many Christian workers and helped them over difficult places.

> There is one person in your church
>   Who knows your preacher's life.
> She's wept and smiled and prayed with him.
>   And that's your preacher's wife!
>
> She knows one prophet's weakest point,
>   And knows his greatest power;
> She's heard him speak in trumpet tone,
>   In his great triumph hour.
>
> She's heard him groaning in his soul,
>   When bitter raged the strife,

As hand in his she knelt with him —
    For she's a preacher's wife.

You tell your tales of prophets brave,
    Who walked across the world
And changed the course of history
    By burning words they hurled.

And I will tell how back of them
    Some women lived their lives,
Who wept with them and smiled with them;
    They were the preachers' wives!

Shortly after the Broadcast began over a quarter of a century ago there came a day when I was very discouraged. I walked the floor saying, "What is the use. We cannot go on this way." My wife suddenly realized that the Devil was trying to get both of us discouraged, and she said she would not give in. She went to be alone with God and to search the Scriptures for a message from Him. He gave her this verse from Job: "Though he slay me, yet will I trust in him." This was what God used to lead us out of that period of despondency. Let us not be too hard on Elijah for becoming discouraged. There can be company which is not companionship. A person can sometimes be more lonely in a crowd than in a desert. We need more than the presence of human beings to help us; we need human hearts to sympathize with us.

When Elijah set the Lord before him, he faced the foe whether man or Devil without fear. But the moment he forgot God and turned to circumstances things changed. He looked at the danger and lost his courage. Centuries later Peter did the same thing. As long as he looked at the Lord he walked on the water and was not afraid. The moment he looked at the waves he became afraid and began to sink.

Someone reading this may be living under difficult circumstances. Perhaps it is a wife who has lived with an ungodly husband whose temper flares up constantly. Perhaps you feel you cannot take it any longer. Look to Jesus instead of the circumstances that are affecting you so badly and the Lord will give you strength. Trust Him to save that husband of yours.

Or it may be you are living in some situation that you could not avoid, and yet you feel it is impossible to continue on in it. "Turn your eyes upon Jesus, Look full in His wonderful face; And the things of earth will grow strangely dim In the light of His glory and grace."

God looked on His servant, Elijah, with kindness. And because of it He provided food for him. The Lord did not forget him. He followed him everywhere. Elijah learned as we should learn: "He (God) hath not dealt with us after our sins; nor rewarded us according to our iniquities. For as the heaven is high above the earth, so great is his mercy toward them that fear him. As far as the east is from the west, so far hath he removed our transgressions from us. Like as a father pitieth his children, so the Lord pitieth them that fear him. For he knoweth our frame; he remembereth that we are dust" (Ps. 103:10-14).

The message of the following poem may speak to your heart as it has to mine:

> Hast thou been hungry, child of mine?
>   I, too, have needed bread.
> For forty days I tasted naught
>   Till by the angels fed.
> Hast thou been thirsty?
>   On the cross I suffered thirst for thee;
> I have promised to supply thy need
>   My child, come unto me.
>
> Perhaps thy way is weary oft,
>   Thy feet grow tired and lame.
> I wearied when I reached the well,
>   I suffered just the same.
> And when I bore the heavy cross
>   I fainted 'neath the load.
> And so I have promised rest to all
>   Who walk the weary road.
>
> Does Satan sometimes buffet thee
>   And tempt thy soul to sin?

Do faith and hope and love grow weak
  Are doubts and fears within?
Remember I was tempted thrice
  By this same foe of thine,
But he could not resist the Word
  Nor conquer power divine.

When thou art sad and tears fall fast,
  My heart goes out to thee
For I wept o'er Jerusalem,
  The place so dear to me.
And when I came to Lazarus' tomb I wept,
  My heart was sore.
I will comfort thee when thou dost weep
  'Til sorrow all is o'er.

Do hearts prove false when thine is true?
  I know that bitter dart;
I was betrayed by one I loved,
  I died of a broken heart.
I loved my own, they loved me not;
  My heart was lonely, too.
I'll never leave thee child of mine
  My loving heart is true.

Art thou discouraged in thy work?
  Does misery seem vain?
I ministered midst unbelief
  With those of greed of gain.
They would not hearken to My voice
  But scoffed with one accord,
Your labor never is in vain
  If done unto the Lord.

So have courage, then, My faithful one;
  I suffered all the way.
Thy sensitive and loving heart
  I understand today.
Whate'er thy grief, whate'er thy care
  Just bring it unto Me.

Yea, in thy day of trouble, call;
I will deliver thee!

Elijah had lost hope of seeing the people of Israel return to the Lord. Thus life no longer was attractive to him. When hope is gone life is not worth living. Perhaps it seemed to Elijah that the Lord had given up the work also, but this was not the case. The Lord did not answer the prayer of His discouraged servant when he asked to die.

The present world has no answer to the turmoil and strife going on in its midst but the church is not without hope. Our hope lies in the coming of our Lord. This we must never lose sight of.

GOD'S KINDNESS TO HIS SERVANT

We learn from the New Testament: "There hath no temptation taken you but such as is common to man: but God is faithful, who will not suffer [permit] you to be tempted above that ye are able; but will with the temptation also make a way to escape, that ye may be able to bear it" (I Cor. 10:13). Perhaps we think our testings are different than those experienced by others, but such is not the case. They are common to man. Circumstances may differ for us, but the tests are the same. Not all of us may run from someone like Jezebel, but we are subject to fear and discouragement regardless of the cause.

How comforting to realize that God knows us intimately. The Psalmist declared long ago: "Like as a father pitieth his children, so the Lord pitieth them that fear him. For he knoweth our frame; he remembereth that we are dust" (Ps. 103:13,14). The Lord will either lighten the burden or He will increase our strength, so that we can bear it.

Another promise of great encouragement to me personally is II Timothy 2:12,13: "If we suffer, we shall also reign with him: if we deny him, he also will deny us: If we believe not, yet he abideth faithful: he cannot deny himself." Elijah failed temporarily to exercise faith, but God did not abandon His servant. God is faithful to His own.

He did not remove the wicked queen Jezebel then and there. Neither did He do some mighty work in Israel. He did, however, make a way of escape for His dejected servant, giving him the strength he needed.

God's eye had followed every step that Elijah had taken. He did not love the prophet less than when he stood in victory on Mount Carmel. God's love is not based on our ability. He will not fail us at any time. His promise is, "I will never leave thee, nor forsake thee. So that we may boldly say, The Lord is my helper, and I will not fear what man shall do unto me" (Heb. 13:5,6).

God does not condone or encourage wrong in a believer's life. He did not approve of Elijah's wish for death as a means of rest. But God felt for His child, and gave him the bodily help he needed. God gave His beloved sleep just as the Psalmist said He would. Elijah found that though weeping may endure for a night, joy comes in the morning.

Good, wholesome, restful sleep is a blessing from God. What healing and strength lie in becoming unconscious for a time to the things around us. God set a divine watch over His servant, and the mind so recently agitated and the heart so filled with fear were quieted and given peace.

What do we do in wakeful night hours? Someone asked me that one time. For myself, one of the first things I love to do is to start praying. Sometimes I recite some of the Scriptures God has put into my heart. There are occasions when that is not sufficient, so I arise and go to my study and take my Bible and spend an hour or more in it. There have been times when I have spent four or five hours in this manner, depending upon what God was seeking to do in my heart.

These have always been precious times. I found that God awakened me that He might speak to me and deal with my soul in a way that He could not at other times.

This is what He did for Elijah. "And as he lay and slept under the juniper tree, behold, then an angel touched him, and said unto him, Arise and eat. And he looked, and, behold, there was a cake baked on the coals, and a cruse of water at his head. And he did eat and drink, and laid him down again. And the angel of the Lord came again the second time, and touched him, and said, Arise and eat; because the journey is too great for thee" (I Kings 19:5-7).

Ministry of Angels

There was still a great distance that Elijah had to go, but God watched over this man as he slept the sleep of sorrow. He was not forsaken but was provided for through rest and food for a journey that would yet cover many miles. Here we have a demonstration of the ministry of angels for those who are the elect of the Lord. We must remember that there is a difference between those who do not fear the Lord and are presumptuous, and Elijah who, though he ran for his life, did not run away from God. God's tender care of such is expressed through the ministry of angels who are servants of those who are heirs of salvation. The same angels who delight to witness God's majesty and greatness also enjoy ministering to God's saints on the earth.

This action on the part of God is typical of His nature as the God of grace. He takes no account of our worthiness or unworthiness. His grace is free and sovereign. He loves His own, and He loves them to the end.

Can you imagine an angel doing such a lowly task as cooking a meal for a discouraged saint of God, when that angel's regular assignment was to stand in the presence of Almighty God and see Him in His majesty and glory? There was no grumbling on the part of this messenger — he loved to do what he did.

When Lot was living in Sodom it was an angel that came to warn him and to get him out from that wicked and doomed city. Daniel was cast into the lions' den but an angel was with him, sent of God to shut the mouths of the ferocious beasts.

When Lazarus the beggar died, angels carried him into Abraham's bosom. When Peter was cast into prison and the authorities planned to put him to death, it was an angel that came by night, awakened him, cast off his chains, and opened the gates of the prison for him. It was an angel that stood by Paul when the ship he was on was about to go to pieces, and assured the apostle that God was going to give the life of every person on board into his hands.

This truth of the ministry of angels is wonderful to consider. God has assigned an angel to each of His own. We are engaged in a spiritual warfare with evil forces in the heavenlies and are adequately provided with the help sufficient for victory.

Angels play an important role with regard to children. We read in Matthew 18:10: "Take heed that ye despise not one of these little ones; for I say unto you, That in heaven their angels do always behold the face of my Father which is in heaven." God has assigned a special angel to each child. This is a most remarkable statement but true because God says so.

The Psalmist wrote: "For he shall give his angels charge over thee, to keep thee in all thy ways." This is Psalm 91:11, and was written concerning the man who dwells in the secret place of the Most high, the man who fears God.

Another precious promise is in Psalm 34:7: "The angel of the Lord encampeth round about them that fear him, and delivereth them." This is provision made by God. Angels are sent to minister with God's purposes in view. It is no wonder, then, that God sent an angel to minister to His servant Elijah and prepare him for a long journey he had to take. The prophet had set his heart on going down to Mount Horeb, the same mountain on which Moses had met God. Perhaps Elijah thought of Moses and his experience when he presented himself to the children of Israel and they rejected him. Then it was he had to flee from Egypt and go deep into the desert; but that was where God met him. This is what Elijah apparently was looking for also.

There are times when each of us feels that a different environment would make things easier for us. We will see, in Elijah's case, what a change in environment did for him, though he could have had the same experience if he had stayed right in Israel. God did not forsake him. Elijah needed spiritual refreshing. He needed to go aside from the duties of life for a while and be alone with the Lord. Our Saviour did this quite often, going off into a mountain to pray.

God allowed his servant to take this long, hard journey across the desert, and in grace provided for him and accompanied him. Whether or not Elijah was in the direct will of God at this time, his heart motive was certainly that of seeking to put God first. The Lord did not forsake him, and He will not forsake us.

We read in verse 8 of I Kings 19 that Elijah "arose, and did eat and drink, and went in the strength of that meat forty days and forty nights unto Horeb the mount of God." Again Elijah experienced the superhuman strength provided by the Lord. This is something He can do either with much or with little. The Lord Jesus fed thousands of people with only five loaves and two small fish. While in the desert the Israelites did not have the means of making clothes or shoes, yet God so provided that their clothing and their shoes did not wear out in all that time.

He Giveth More Grace*

He giveth more grace when the burdens grow greater;
He sendeth more strength when the labors increase.
To added affliction He addeth His mercy;
To multiplied trials, His multiplied peace.

When we have exhausted our store of endurance,
When our strength has failed ere the day is half done,
When we reach the end of our hoarded resources,
Our Father's full giving is only begun.

His love has no limit, His grace has no measure,
His pow'r has no boundary known unto men;
For out of His infinite riches in Jesus,
He giveth, and giveth, and giveth again!

                                        —Annie Johnson Flint

Like Elijah we all come to times of discouragement. None of us are immune. Pastors often find themselves targets of the enemy in this respect. They preach their hearts out for the Lord but see little response, if any, in the hearts of the hearers. Lesser things begin to take the time of the members of their congregation. Sunday night meetings dwindle. The prayer meetings hold little interest, and so far as going after the unsaved, the average Christian seems to have lost that vision.

Regardless of the cause of our discouragement let us learn from this experience of Elijah that God is never discouraged.

---

*Copyright. Reproduced by permission, Evangelical Publishers, Toronto, Canada.

He never gives up. When God has laid the responsibility for some work or obligation upon us, let us learn not to give up either.

Sometimes God's plans do not coincide with what we think they should be. Not all His plans are short range; many of them are long range. Though he did not realize it at the time, Elijah was fitting into a part of God's long-range plan in connection with Israel.

God's Love for Elijah

At the time of his discouragement Elijah was the recipient of the love of God in a very special way. He did not rebuke his tired and depressed servant but provided food and rest and protection and comfort and strength by an angel.

If he had not learned it before, Elijah learned then, that God's love is constant. Perhaps he may have feared that he had forfeited that love by running away from Jezebel and her threats; but regardless of his feelings, God loved him. The love of God never changes though our awareness of it does. Just as the sun can go behind clouds so that it is not seen or the rotation of the earth brings on night, the sun continues to shine.

The love of God is like that. We may not always be aware of the evidences of God's love but it surrounds us. The circumstances of life may surround us like a cloud or like the mantle of night, but God's love is not one whit changed. It is still with us.

Elijah also learned that God's love is at times manifested in a very special way to meet special needs in our lives. There is no mention of an angel when Elijah was cared for at the Brook Cherith. No angel is mentioned concerning his stay with the widow at Zarephath. Something more was needed after this fall by Elijah. God has no pleasure in sin. His holiness is offended by it, but He remembers our frame. In Elijah's case, in order to assure the prophet that he was still loved and to bring him to the place of repentance and usefulness, God sent an angel to help him.

We can see this in Peter's experience. After he had denied

the Lord three times he wept in bitterness of spirit at his own weakness and carnality. The Lord did not leave him in that condition. The women who went to the tomb on the morning of the resurrection were told by a young man clothed in a long white garment: "Be not affrighted: Ye seek Jesus of Nazareth, which was crucified: he is risen; he is not here: behold the place where they laid him. But go your way, tell his disciples AND PETER that he goeth before you into Galilee: there shall ye see him, as he said unto you" (Mark 16:6,7). The very fact that Peter was especially mentioned here was a message of love to him. God's love is a giving type of love. Our affection and consideration for people may be shaken by circumstances because basically we are selfish. God's love is just the opposite; it is constantly giving of itself and does not change.

It was while we were yet sinners that Christ died for us. The Lord went out after the wandering sheep and carried it home. When the prodigal returned, the fatted calf was prepared for him. All this shows the special love of God for the sinner. God hates our sin but He yearns over us with tender, unchanging love. God who gave His only begotten Son for us will allow nothing to separate us from His love.

The Williams Translation of Romans 8 beginning with verse 31 reads: "What are we then to say to facts like these? If God is for us, who can be against us? Since He did not spare His own Son but gave Him up for us all, will He not with Him graciously give us everything else? Who can bring any charge against those whom God has chosen? It is God who declared them in right standing; who can condemn them? Christ Jesus who died, or rather, who was raised from the dead, is now at God's right hand, and is actually pleading for us. Who can separate us from Christ's love? Can suffering or misfortune or persecution or hunger or destitution or danger or the sword? As the Scripture says: 'For your sake we are being put to death the livelong day; We are treated like sheep to be slaughtered.' And yet in all these things we keep on gloriously conquering through Him who loved us. For I have full assurance that neither death nor life nor angels nor principalities nor the present nor the future nor evil forces above or beneath, nor anything else in all creation, will be able to separate us from the love of God as shown in Christ Jesus our Lord."

The inspired apostle closes the 11th chapter of Romans with these words: "How fathomless the depths of God's resources, wisdom, and knowledge! How unsearchable His decisions, and how mysterious His methods! For who has ever understood the thoughts of the Lord, or has ever been His adviser? Or who has ever advanced God anything to have Him pay him back? For from Him everything comes, through Him everything lives, and for Him everything exists. Glory to Him forever! Amen" (vv. 33-36).

The third fact Elijah learned concerning the love of God is that His love endures. Using an angel as His messenger God first provided Elijah with food. He had been traveling for a long time in the desert. After he slept for awhile the angel awakened him and gave him a meal. Then after a good long rest, possibly early in the morning, the angel came again and awakened Elijah and told him to arise and eat because the journey was too long for him. There is no let up to God's love. It suffers long and is kind. It endures all things and will never fail. After he had rested and was refreshed Elijah was ready for the next phase of his ministry.

God offers us after our day's task is over food that is more than physical. In the morning before our day's journey begins He provides fresh bread from His Word for our nourishment and strength.

This is spoken of time and again in the Scriptures. Isaiah commented on this: "Hast thou not known? hast thou not heard, that the everlasting God, the Lord, the Creator of the ends of the earth, fainteth not, neither is weary? there is no searching of his understanding. He giveth power to the faint; and to them that have no might he increaseth strength. Even the youths shall faint and be weary, and the young men shall utterly fall: But they that wait upon the Lord shall renew their strength; they shall mount up with wings as eagles; they shall run, and not be weary; and they shall walk, and not faint" (40:28-31).

Elijah arose and ate and went in the strength of the food provided for forty days and forty nights. When he reached Horeb, the mount of God, "he came thither unto a cave, and lodged there; and, behold, the word of the Lord came to him, and he said unto him, What doest thou here, Elijah?" (I Kings 19:9). This was a question designed to stir up Elijah's thinking with regard to his present situation and future ministry.

This was a long distance from the scenes of his labors in Israel. He had traveled some 100 miles to where God found him under the juniper tree, and from there he had traveled about 200 miles more through the desert in order to reach the place where Moses had stayed while a fugitive from Egypt. Perhaps Elijah felt that in this place he would be able to speak with God as Moses had done many years before.

Elijah was not in the will of God when he fled from Jezebel, but it looks as though the Lord directed his steps to Horeb in order to bring him to a place of usefulness again. Nevertheless, he had all of these hundreds of miles to retrace. God is sovereign in His grace and did not forsake His servant in his hour of need.

CHAPTER TEN

ELIJAH AT HOREB

The distance traveled to Horeb was some 200 miles, and under normal conditions could have been covered in seven or eight days. Why it took him longer we are not told, but it reminds us of Israel wandering in the desert for 40 years to complete a journey that could have been made in a few weeks.

As Elijah approached the lofty heights of this great mountain he must have been reminded of the remarkable dealings of God with Moses and Israel at this place. It was here that God met Moses at the burning bush. Then later when Israel was liberated and was on its way to Canaan it was here that God gave them the law. This was the same mountain where Moses interceded for his people that they might not be destroyed. Here was witnessed the victory over Amalek and the miracle of water coming from the rock. Though God gave Elijah no commandment to go to Horeb, yet he must have been directed there by the secret providence of God.

We need to remind ourselves of what the Bible teaches concerning God's watch-care of His children. In one place we read, "A man's heart deviseth his way: but the Lord directeth his steps" (Prov. 16:9). In another place God says, "Man's goings are of the Lord; how can a man then understand his own way?" (Prov. 20:24). The hearts of men are under God's control, for Proverbs 21:1,2 says, "The king's heart is in the hand of the Lord, as the rivers of water: he turneth it whithersoever he will. Every way of a man is right in his own eyes: but the Lord pondereth the hearts." God knew the heart of Elijah and He knew that Elijah was still vitally concerned about heavenly things and the honor of his God.

It was while he was alone in the cave, possibly thinking

that he was forsaken, that God asked him, "What doest thou here, Elijah?" God was right there with him in spite of all the fear and strain that Elijah had labored under.

The passage says that the "word of the Lord" came to Elijah. This reminds us of John 1:1 which reads: "In the beginning was the Word, and the Word was with God, and the Word was God." This could have been none other than the Second Person in the Trinity, the Lord Jesus Christ himself who spoke with Elijah.

The question, "What doest thou here, Elijah?" was an appeal to the conscience. This type of question leads to self-examination. It is well for us to open our hearts to the Lord to let Him raise this same question with us. None can escape the ever-present inquiry of the Lord's examination. He has a right to know when He asks, "What are you doing here?"

We learn from Proverbs 15:3: "The eyes of the Lord are in every place, beholding the evil and the good." A further truth is added concerning this in II Chronicles 16:9: "For the eyes of the Lord run to and fro throughout the whole earth, to shew himself strong in the behalf of them whose heart is perfect toward him."

Elijah's answer to God's inquiry was very frank. He did not seek to evade the issues. His words are, "I have been very jealous for the Lord God of hosts: for the children of Israel have forsaken thy covenant, thrown down thine altars, and slain thy prophets with the sword; and I, even I only, am left; and they seek my life, to take it away" (I Kings 19:10).

Elijah admitted his thoughts of his own hopelessness. Everything he said was true, but he did not know the truth about everything in connection with his own life. He was not aware of God's far-reaching plan for himself and Israel. He had to learn that God does not necessarily fulfill His whole plan in the lifetime of one man. One servant may add one part to God's work and another, another part, and it is all of these parts put together that make up the whole. This was what God was getting ready to teach Elijah.

Yet, how many of us could answer with ready candor God's question, "What are you doing here?" How do we rate

as to our heart's intensity in the things of God — are we cold,
or are we hot, or are we lukewarm?

God's reply to Elijah's answer was, "Go forth, and stand
upon the mount before the Lord. And, behold, the Lord passed
by, and a great and strong wind rent the mountains, and brake
in pieces the rocks before the Lord; but the Lord was not in the
wind: and after the wind an earthquake; but the Lord was not
in the earthquake: And after the earthquake a fire; but the
Lord was not in the fire: and after the fire a still small voice"
(I Kings 19:11,12).

What would our answer be to such a command as "Go
forth. Stand before the Lord." Too many of us are imprisoned
by ourselves in our own thoughts. Too many of us take a nega-
tive approach to these deep and serious things in life. We talk
about the sins of the world, its depravity and wickedness but
what are we doing to reach men for Christ?

Today we speak about our nation going to the dogs. We
criticize the world and look with displeasure at our young
people. What do we do about it all? Like Elijah, we need a new
vision of the Lord. We need to come out of the cave of darkness
and stand before God.

The next few words in this chapter tell us, "The Lord
passed by." Elijah remained in the cave during the time of this
great storm and earthquake and fire, all of which demonstrated
the power of God. This was very much like the time when God
spoke to Moses on the mount and the people of Israel were
terrified at the demonstration of God's power in the elements.

God's Grace

God, however, did not speak in the wind, or in the earthquake, or in the fire. He did not speak to Elijah from the standpoint of the law, but rather from the standpoint of grace. The
still small voice speaks of Mount Zion not with the legal requirements of Sinai, but with the generous gifts of God's grace.

When Elijah heard God speak he "wrapped his face in his
mantle, and went out, and stood in the entering in of the cave.
And, behold, there came a voice unto him, and said, What doest
thou here, Elijah?" Not the law, but grace, broke his heart. It is

the goodness of God that leads us to repentance. Once more Elijah repeated what we have already quoted from verse 11, but now the Lord is ready to recommission him.

All was not lost as Elijah was brought to realize. Though God spoke through the great demonstrations of nature, He was still going to speak to His people in grace. The thunder and the fire and the earthquake brought fear, but only grace brings true revival.

Too often we seek great demonstrations, crowds and all kinds of activity but God brings about revival through dealing with the individual soul and heart in the quietness of grace. The thunders of judgment are necessary, but the still small voice of the gospel is that which penetrates the hearts of men.

In a very real sense Elijah had been a voice of thunder and fire to Israel. Like John the Baptist who later in Israel's history thundered the message of repentance, Elijah had spoken out a warning to a nation in rebellion against God. He was recommissioned to still speak in that manner and, yet, at the same time, there was the promise of grace for those who would respond.

Elijah Provided For

God spoke to Elijah as He did in order to prepare him for a new commission. Though it was many years later that Peter penned his epistle, what he wrote will help us as we think about Elijah. The truth given by Peter most certainly was in God's mind with regard to His servant of old. "According as his divine power hath given unto us all things that pertain unto life and godliness, through the knowledge of him that hath called us to glory and virtue [energy, efficiency]" (II Pet. 1:3). God never leaves us without properly equipping us for the work we are to do.

We can apply these things to Elijah and find God saying in effect: "Elijah, you need not be despondent or run from Me. There is no need for you to be afraid. I am your God and have given you all that is essential and necessary for life. Jezebel will not be able to take your life. I have made ample provision for your spiritual growth and development. Remember the blessings of bygone days, the brook and the ravens, the barrel and the cruse of oil, the fire that fell from heaven when you asked for it and the rain that you brought through your prayers. Remember, Elijah, I am the God who made all of this possible. I am your God and have provided everything you need."

Perhaps we have felt like Elijah and said, "What is the use?" Perhaps we have given the best of our lives to something for the Lord and feel that we have been left stranded. Perhaps we feel the enemy is seeking to destroy all phases of Christianity and belief in the true God, and is after our soul, too. Perhaps we feel we are the only one left of all God's people. If so, we need to be reminded, as was Elijah, that God still has 7000 who have not bowed their knee to Baal. And God still is the Almighty God. He is still on His throne. Men cannot dethrone Him, no matter how hard they try. All we need for life and godliness and Christian service is found in Him.

Perhaps we have tried hard to overcome temptations and rise above our testings. Perhaps we have fought against the overwhelming odds of modernism in our church. Perhaps we have done so and have found few if any standing with us, and we are about ready to give up our belief in the fundamental things of the Word of God. Do not give up, God is still in control of this world and this universe.

Perhaps we have tried hard to live for the Lord and have failed. Perhaps we fail today as we failed yesterday and the day before and are asking: "What's the use?" Friends, let us come out of the cave of darkness and listen to the still small voice of God. He tells us that He has given all that pertains to life and godliness. Every provision has been made for us.

Again Peter speaks to us: "Wherefore the rather, brethren, give diligence to make your calling and election sure: for if ye do these things, ye shall never fall" (II Pet. 1:10). The word "calling" refers to the fact that God has called us out of this world of sin and provided for us everything necessary to live a holy, godly life just as we read in verse 3. We are called out from the ways of men and from the rules and regulations of man-made systems to find our life in Christ. The fact that

God has called us means that He has invited us to share His nature and power and everything that He wishes us to have.

In fact, God has promised to come and live His life in us so that He is our strength and our moral force. This is our calling and we need to make it a confirmed thing in our lives. We need to apply it by faith. To "make it sure" does not mean we put it into a safe place for keeping or put a padlock on it. It simply means that we accept it and act upon it because God has provided it.

The word "election" is based on the sovereign will of God and the power and the purpose of God. The same truth is seen where we are told that we have been chosen in Him. God for example, chose Abraham from all the rest of the people in Chaldea. It was not because Abraham was good in himself but because God decided Abraham was the man He wanted. The same Lord chose Isaac instead of Ishmael and Jacob instead of Esau. He has chosen us also for a special work and wants to see that fulfilled in us.

This was what Elijah found concerning his service. He found he was chosen to be the voice of thunder and of fire and of condemnation to Israel. This is what God had chosen him to be, and though the prophet would not see the fruit of it in his time, nevertheless, there would be fruitage from it.

It was because he knew that he had been called to a certain work and that he could not perform that work in himself that Paul said, "That I might know him [Christ], and the power of his resurrection." Paul wanted the Lord to live His life in him. That was why the apostle decided to forget the things that were behind. He wanted to lay hold of that for which Christ had laid hold of him. So he reached out to those things which were ahead and pressed on toward the mark for the prize of the high calling of God in Christ Jesus. He saw this calling as an invitation to accept Christ as his very life, a life to be lived in him anew and afresh from day to day.

Elijah Recommissioned

When God spoke in the still small voice to Elijah, the prophet's heart broke. The God of Israel asked this man to let

Him be his life. He said that He had chosen him to be His voice of thunder and not to be concerned about the fruit. That was God's business.

As the grace of God broke upon Elijah, he hid his face. But he listened to the Lord when He said: "Go, return on thy way to the wilderness of Damascus: and when thou comest, anoint Hazael to be king over Syria" (I Kings 19:15). This man was going to be a rod to chastise Israel and Elijah was to inaugurate this work.

He was also to anoint "Jehu the son of Nimshi" to be king over Israel. What Hazael left Jehu was to finish.

The third part of the commission was that Elijah was to anoint Elisha the son of Shaphat to be a prophet in his place. Elijah's work was not yet finished but God had chosen a particular person to be Elijah's understudy and carry on the work which he began.

Laborers Together

The fact that no one man sees all the plan of God and no one man sees all the fruit of his labors in his lifetime so far as God's work is concerned is taught very clearly in Hebrews 11. Beginning with verse 37 the writer says concerning the great heroes of the faith: "They were stoned, they were sawn asunder, were tempted, were slain with the sword: they wandered about in sheepskins and goatskins; being destitute, afflicted, tormented; (Of whom the world was not worthy:) they wandered in deserts, and in mountains, and in dens and caves of the earth. And these all, having obtained a good report through faith, received not the promise." Though they were all faithful and true to the Lord they did not see the complete fruitage of their labors in their lifetime. The record continues: "God having provided some better thing for us, that they without us should not be made perfect." It takes all of God's people from the beginning of time to the very end to fulfill all that He has planned.

Over a period of years God adds this member and that member to do a particular task. This should keep us from discouragement when we fail to see fruit to any great extent

142 ELIJAH, A MAN OF LIKE NATURE

in our lifetime. It may be fruit for which we have labored hard and long and because of seeing little of it think God has not worked through us.

The fact of the matter is if we are in the will of God, He is working through us. What we need to recognize is that we do one particular task the fruit of which we see by faith but possibly never by sight. This is what the men of faith did according to Hebrews 11. They did not see the fruit in their generation but they did see it afar off through faith. Like them we need to learn to fit into God's plan for us, and we will find out that He is coordinating the work of all His children into one great master plan.

As we have noted before, Elijah was not consciously running from God, neither was he embittered. He was disappointed and depressed because he saw no national revival on Israel's part. He did not see the future as God saw it. Others would reap where he had sown.

How true that is in the experience of many today. Pastors labor hard in seeking to win the lost for Christ and perhaps see little fruit. Then an evangelist is called in and he reaps the harvest and often the credit. It is as Paul tells us, one plants, another waters, but it is God who gives the increase. He is also keeping the books and will apportion the rewards properly and justly.

This is true with regard to our work also. We do not see a great deal of the fruit that results from our preaching but we do see some. Moreover, we rejoice when those who are saved through the Broadcast ministry join local churches where the gospel is preached, and develop and grow under a local ministry. It takes many hands to do the work of the Lord.

Once Elijah was restored through the will of God to fellowship with the Lord he was recommissioned and told to "Go, return on thy way to the wilderness of Damascus" (I Kings 19:15). The word "return" is the same word as "retrace." Elijah had to go back the way he had come in order to fulfill this commission. He had a long journey ahead of him.

This is the procedure that must be followed by anyone who has temporarily stepped out of the direct will of God. There must be a retracing of the life and a going back to the place where God's directive will can be followed once more.

Take the case of Abraham, for example. According to the 12th chapter of Genesis Abraham was instructed to dwell in the land of Canaan, but when a famine struck he went down into Egypt. He stepped out of the direct will of God in doing this and found himself in deep trouble with Pharaoh. The Lord delivered him and sent him back to the land of promise, so Abraham went up out of Egypt and "went on his journeys from the south even to Beth-el, unto the place where his tent had been at the beginning, between Beth-el and Hai; Unto the place of the altar, which he had made there at the first: and there Abram called on the name of the Lord" (Gen. 13:3,4).

Abraham lapsed in faith again at Gerar and had to be recalled from that place into the direct will of God. He had no fellowship with the Lord as long as he was out of the place God had designated was to be his dwelling place.

Abraham's grandson Jacob went through the same kind of experience. Because of some things he did he had to flee from the home of his parents and was gone from the land for many years. Then God called him back to Beth-el but Jacob stayed at Shechem where some very sad experiences took place. Then again God called him to go to Beth-el and dwell there, "and make there an altar unto God, that appeared unto thee when thou fleddest from the face of Esau thy brother. Then Jacob said unto his household, and to all that were with him, Put away the strange gods that are among you, and be clean, and change your garments: And let us arise, and go up to Beth-el; and I will make there an altar unto God, who answered me in the day of my distress" (Gen. 35:1-3). He had to go back to the place where he left the revealed will of God before he could make a fresh start.

The same principle is taught in the Book of Revelation. To the Church at Ephesus our Saviour said, "Nevertheless I have somewhat against thee, because thou hast left thy first love. Remember therefore from whence thou art fallen, and repent [turn around], and do the first works; or else I will come unto thee quickly, and will remove thy candlestick out of his place, except thou repent" (2:4,5).

Peter had to retrace his steps after he denied the Lord and was recommissioned. The prodigal had to go from the far country to his father's house. There had to be a retracing of his steps. This is not always easy to the flesh.

Elijah's journey would take him back through the desert, on through Jezebel's homeland, and all the way up to Damascus. Had he stayed at Carmel and been given the instructions he was given while at Mount Horeb, he would have had only about 100 miles to go to Damascus. Added to that was now the distance from the Mount of God.

The Word tells us: "He that covereth his sin shall not prosper, but whoso forsaketh them [leaves them and returns to the Lord] he shall find mercy."

Part of Elijah's recommissioning was to anoint Hazael king over Syria. This man was to be God's rod of chastisement on Israel. This anointing was not performed by Elijah, but by Elisha who was Elijah's understudy. And when this prophet stood before Hazael he wept, and when asked why, he replied, "Because I know the evil that thou wilt do unto the children of Israel: their strong holds wilt thou set on fire, and their young men wilt thou slay with the sword, and wilt dash their children, and rip up their women with child." Hazael was like a tornado wherever he went. He represented the storm and the destruction of the fierce winds. This was the answer to the complaint of Elijah concerning Israel's backsliding.

He was also to anoint Jehu who was to bring judgment on the house of Ahab. This anointing was likewise done not directly by Elijah but through Elisha. Jehu was like an earthquake, shaking the house of Ahab from within. Jezebel was thrown down from a window of her home and her body eaten by dogs. Jehu slew 70 sons of Ahab in one day and made public display of their heads. He rooted out Baal worship, and this was the answer of God to Elijah's complaint concerning the worship of Baal and the household of Ahab.

The third part of his commission was to anoint Elisha in his place. This speaks of the power of the Word which was like a two-edged sword. This was an answer to Elijah's complaint when he thought that no one was left as a prophet of Jehovah. The fire Elijah had kindled would continue through the ministry of Elisha.

God uses various instruments to do His work. Hazael, the king of Syria, brought ruthless judgment upon Israel. Jehu became a scourge to the house of Ahab and to the followers of Baal. Elisha, by his use of the Word of God and the power of God, slew the enemies of the Lord and comforted His people.

God sometimes uses wicked men to discipline His own children, but when these men overstep the boundaries God has set for them, judgment falls on their heads also.

God also reminded Elijah that there were 7000 persons left who had not bowed to Baal. This was all in God's dealing through the still small voice of grace. It brought comfort to the prophet's heart. It assured him that the good work he had begun would be consummated under the hand of God and in God's time. Elijah did not see the fruit in his day, but he was promised a fruitful harvest for the future.

THE CALL OF ELISHA

We must introduce Elisha into Elijah's life at this time in order to show how God works first through one man and then another. This does not mean that God works in the same identical way through each one but in fulfilling His plan He uses each person in a particular way though the plan is the same. We have already learned that Elijah was commissioned to anoint Elisha in his place. Contrary to Elijah's thought there were 7000 who had not bowed their knee to Baal. A very literal translation of what God said to him with regard to this is, "I will keep me seven thousand, those who have not bowed their knee to Baal, or whose mouth has not kissed him" (I Kings 19:18). Elisha was of this number and God directed His call and anointing for just the right time in Elijah's life and program.

Elijah was also to anoint Hazael to be king of Syria and Jehu to be king over Israel. Only one of these, that is, the anointing of Elisha, did Elijah actually perform. The other two were anointed by Elisha when he took over Elijah's ministry.

The outstanding factor concerning the older prophet's life was his obedience to God. He left Horeb to do God's bidding.

Like him, if we are going to be in God's work and have His blessing, we must be obedient. Men like D. L. Moody were used because they were obedient. The great evangelist's life verse was one that spoke of obedience. He determined he would be obedient to God regardless of what God told him to do.

It does not matter whether men understand us or not or think we are even sane or not as long as we are true to God. Obedience to Him is the important thing.

The meaning of these two men's names is instructive. Elijah means "my God is Jehovah." Elisha on the other hand means "my God is salvation." Just as the names meant different things though both men honored God, so their life work differed though their life work was serving God.

Elijah was like Moses in that he vindicated the divine holiness of God. He was an ambassador of wrath against lawlessness and rebellion. Elisha was an evangelist, a representative of God's loving-kindness. The main thrust of his ministry was not to threaten or terrify but to woo, to persuade and to convert men. Both men received their message from God but the message for each differed. This was God-ordained. Some men are called of God to give a message of condemnation and of judgment while others, like the still small voice, speak more of God's grace. The Holy Spirit has absolute sovereignty in giving gifts to men and in choosing whom He will to perform specific tasks.

We learn from I Corinthians 12: "Now there are diversities of gifts, but the same Spirit. And there are differences of administrations, but the same Lord [different ways in which things can be done under the direction of the same Spirit]. And there are diversities of operations, but it is the same God which worketh all in all. But the manifestation of the Spirit is given to every man to profit withal. . . . But all these worketh that one and the selfsame Spirit, dividing to every man severally as he will" (vv. 4-11).

This whole chapter in I Corinthians shows that the body of Christ is like a human body with many members and no two members have the same identical task. Our responsibility is to fulfill the task given us by God and not to try to imitate someone else.

Elisha's Background

When Elijah found Elisha he was in a field plowing along with his servants. There were twelve yoke of oxen, twelve plows, eleven servants, and Elisha in charge of the last plow. This indicates that he was not farming just a small place but was a man of substance with a large farm.

The fact that he was with the twelfth yoke of oxen shows that he did not feel himself too important as the proprietor of a large farm to plow alongside his servants. He was a humble man and reminds us that God, according to I Corinthians 1:26, does not call many mighty to do His work.

Elisha was not a man who minded high things. He was the last man in line, humble enough to be in the last row following the plow.

When Elijah found him, he "cast his mantle upon him." The prophet did not have a long talk with him and discuss the various aspects of the work involved. By casting his mantle over Elisha he was simply saying to him that he was God's chosen man and he was to follow Elijah. Elisha understood quite well what was meant.

God exercises the same sovereign right in our lives. He chooses whom He will. In John 15:16 the Lord Jesus said, "Ye have not chosen me, but I have chosen you, and ordained you, that ye should go and bring forth fruit, and that your fruit should remain: that whatsoever ye shall ask of the Father in my name, he may give it you."

The Apostle Paul touches on this same matter in II Corinthians 5: "And all things are of God, who hath reconciled us to himself by Jesus Christ, and hath given to us the ministry of reconciliation; To wit, that God was in Christ, reconciling the world unto himself" (vv. 18,19). This is speaking of service. The choice is not ours; it belongs to God.

Elisha's Response

Elisha's response was immediate. There was no hesitation. It is very likely that he had been burdened of the Lord for quite some time to go into a full-time ministry for Him but did not know how to do it. Furthermore, it was a dangerous matter in that day for anyone to make it known that he was going to follow the Lord. Jezebel's vindictive and cruel spirit was still being manifested, and anyone declaring himself to be a prophet of God would be hunted for their life. Elijah, of course, had been spared, and Elisha did not hold back when he was commissioned.

He immediately left his oxen and ran after Elijah and said he would like to stay behind just a little while in order to make a feast, so that he could say good-bye to his friends and his parents.

He planned a public farewell as a witness to his family and his friends. This was different than the person recorded in the New Testament who was asked to follow the Lord but requested that he might go back and bury his father. What he meant, of course, was that he wanted to stay at home until his father died. He wanted to take care of that area of family responsibility before he followed the Lord. Then it was the Lord Jesus said, "Let the dead bury their dead."

Elisha, however, did not say, "Let me bury my parents," but rather "Let me kiss them good-bye." This was an entirely different situation.

A great New Testament principle concerning this is given in Luke 14:25-27: "And there went great multitudes with him: and he turned, and said unto them, If any man come to me, and hate not his father, and mother, and wife, and children, and brethren, and sisters, yea, and his own life also, he cannot be my disciple. And whosoever doth not bear his cross, and come after me, cannot be my disciple." The word "hate" in this passage does not mean hate in a bad sense. Our Saviour is simply saying that the person who does not put his family in second place and Christ in first place cannot be His disciple. We must love the Lord supremely; if we do we will put even our closest loved ones in a secondary position.

Elijah's answer was, "Go back again: for what have I done to thee?" (v. 20). This was as much as saying to Elisha that he should settle the matter with God, not with Elijah. Many times we feel we have to bring our excuses before men, but when we are right with God we do not have to justify ourselves with men. I think that is what Elijah was saying to Elisha. God was choosing Elisha, so whatever Elisha did about it was to be settled with God and not with his servant.

Elisha made a complete break with his past. He made a complete surrender to God and broke off all ties with the old life. He took the yoke of oxen he had been plowing with — and possibly they were his best—and slew them for the dual purpose of an offering before God on the one hand and a feast for his friends on the other. He made firewood out of the plow and the yokes. Thus a complete sacrifice is evidenced on his part. His friends and neighbors saw him burning all his bridges behind him, cutting off all connections with his former life and ownership of property.

Romans 12:1 says, "I beseech you therefore, brethren, by the mercies of God, that ye present your bodies a living sacrifice, holy, acceptable unto God, which is your reasonable service." Everything we have, according to this, then, belongs to God. In other words, sacrifice speaks of death but this passage speaks of a living sacrifice which indicates that we give ourselves to God to live entirely for Him. If we are to be true servants of the Lord this is the kind of sacrifice involved.

After Elisha had provided a feast for the people and kissed his parents good-bye, he arose and went after Elijah. The older prophet became his spiritual father and Elisha took the humble place of being his servant. He served a man in serving God. This is what Joshua did with regard to Moses, and then God called him to lead the people at Moses' death. This is the method God sometimes follows in giving men their basic training for His service. This is not the only method He follows, but this is the one that was followed in Elisha's case.

ELIJAH ANNOUNCES AHAB'S DOOM

Following the appointment of Elisha there was a period of silence concerning Elijah. Five or six years passed before his ministry brings him to the public eye. He was not inactive during this period, but seems to have been forming schools of the prophets, schools in which the Bible was taught to young men who were in turn to be instructors and teachers of the Word of God. Elijah was a spiritual father and the teacher of many of these young servants of God.

During this same time, there were great wars between Israel and Syria. Ahab took an active part in these and from time to time prophets of lesser stature than that of Elijah appeared briefly on the scene.

Then one day God again roused up Elijah to appear before Ahab to announce that monarch's doom. This was due to a very wicked crime he had committed.

A Terrible Deed

The background of the incident is as follows. In the city of Jezreel, hard by the palace of Ahab, was a vineyard owned by Naboth. The king wanted this vineyard for himself and asked Naboth to sell it. Naboth, who was a God-fearing man, stated that he was forbidden of the Lord to sell the vineyard, for it was his inheritance from his fathers.

Ahab acted like a spoiled child when he returned to his palace. He went to bed and turned away his face from his servants and refused to eat.

When Jezebel, his wife, learned of his sulking and childish behavior, she questioned him to find out its cause. Her cruel but agile mind soon settled on a solution, and she told her husband to arise and be cheerful for the vineyard was as good as his. She put her plan into motion. Through forged letters and false witnesses and a trial that was a mockery, she had Naboth put to death with the sanction of law. Apparently his sons were also murdered at this time though we are not given the particulars concerning their deaths (II Kings 9:26).

Though the scheme was Jezebel's, the guilt was shared by her weak and pouting husband. He had little time to go to Naboth's vineyard and gloat over his new possession before Elijah stood before him. Faithful to the trust committed to him by God, Elijah wasted no time in presenting himself before the King. Ahab's first words to him were, "Hast thou found me, O mine enemy?" (I Kings 21:20).

The prophet replied, "I have found thee: because thou hast sold thyself to work evil in the sight of the Lord" (I Kings 21:20). Jezebel and Ahab may have thought they had covered up their crime quite well, but God had seen what they had done. There was nothing hidden from God's eyes. He neither slumbers nor sleeps. All things are open before Him.

John's description of the Lord Jesus Christ in the Book of the Revelation adds force to this fact. "His eyes were as a flame of fire; And his feet like unto fine brass, as if they burned in a furnace; and his voice as the sound of many waters" (1:14,15). His eyes see all. There is nothing that can be hidden from Him. The darkness is as the day to Him. His eyes are eyes of fire.

God is never mocked. Whatever a man sows he reaps (Gal. 6:7,8). Ahab should have remembered that his sin would find him out. Naboth lay buried under the earth, but the voice of his blood cried to heaven for vengeance. Man may get away with murder before men, but they never get away with anything before God. We read, "For we know him that hath said, Vengeance belongeth unto me, I will recompense, saith the Lord. And again, The Lord shall judge his people. It is a fearful thing to fall into the hands of the living God" (Heb. 10:30,31).

None of us need ever think we will get by with sin. "The eyes of the Lord are in every place, beholding the evil and the good" (Prov. 15:3). A day of reckoning is coming, and God is keeping the record of all events. He does not keep the books because He forgets, but as written evidence to convince any of us who might dispute the truth.

Jeremiah states, "Can any hide himself in secret places that I shall not see him? saith the Lord. Do not I fill heaven and earth? saith the Lord" (23:24). In Job, we read: "For his eyes are upon the ways of man, and he seeth all his goings. There is no darkness, nor shadows of death, where the workers of iniquity may hide themselves" (34:21,22). We can hide nothing from the eyes of God.

God always denounces sin. Ahab was not long in learning of God's displeasure and anger at this terrible deed. God's warnings and denouncing of evil of today are just as clear and definite. To those so-called ministers who do not preach the gospel, Jeremiah says, "Behold, a whirlwind of the Lord is gone forth in fury, even a grievous whirlwind: it shall fall grievously upon the head of the wicked" (23:19). A whirlwind is like a tornado. It is destructive in its force. The prophet continues, "The anger of the Lord shall not return, until he have executed, and till he have performed the thoughts of his heart: in the latter days ye shall consider it perfectly. I have not sent these prophets, yet they ran: I have not spoken to them, yet they prophesied. . . . I have heard what the prophets said, that prophesy lies in my name, saying, I have dreamed, I have dreamed" (Jer. 23:20-25).

Still speaking out against these prophets, the Lord says through Jeremiah: "Is not my word like as a fire? saith the Lord; and like a hammer that breaketh the rock in pieces? Therefore, behold, I am against the prophets, saith the Lord, that steal my words every one from his neighbour. Behold, I am against the prophets, saith the Lord, that use their tongues, and say, He saith" (23:29-31).

There are false prophets today who deny that Jesus Christ is the eternal God and that He came and died for our sins. The same false prophets deny that it is necessary for men to be born again. They try to tickle the ears of their hearers with teachings that are not from God. God says concerning them: "I have not sent them, and I am coming like a whirlwind to judge them."

We can all be sure that our sins will find us out. Adam thought he could hide from God but God found him. Cain murdered Abel, but Abel's blood cried to God from the ground. Achan stole the accursed thing, but God found him out. Ahab, who was jointly responsible with his wife for the murder of Naboth could not escape the eye of God. God found him out. Gehazi, the servant of Elisha, thought he could do something behind Elisha's back that would increase his personal wealth, but God saw his sin and denounced him through the prophet. Ananias and Sapphira thought they could lie to God and He would not see through it, but they were wrong. Let none think they can escape divine retribution for wrong done.

The Scriptures are very clear on this. In Jude 14 and 15, we learn: "Behold, the Lord cometh with ten thousands of his saints, To execute judgment upon all, and to convince all that are ungodly among them of all their ungodly deeds which they have ungodly committed, and of all their hard speeches which ungodly sinners have spoken against him."

Ahab sold himself to work evil in the sight of the Lord and could not get away with it. The Bible declares: "All have sinned, and come short of the glory of God." It also states, "The wages of sin is death; but the gift of God is eternal life through Jesus Christ" (Rom. 6:23). Those who, like Ahab, sell themselves to work evil in the sight of God, will be found out. It is true, that mercy belongs to God but mercy must be applied for. It cannot be earned. There is no means by which we can merit it. The wages of sin is death. It is only through the gift of God that we can receive eternal life through Jesus Christ our Lord.

I have known Christians who have sold themselves to sin, even some Christian leaders, but the Lord warns us: "Know ye not that ye are the temple of God, and that the Spirit of God dwelleth in you? If any man defile the temple of God, him shall God destroy; for the temple of God is holy, which temple ye are" (I Cor. 3:16,17).

Let us not think we have time on our hands to make things right with God. Today is the day of salvation. Or, if you are already saved but need to return to fellowship, now is the time to come back to the Lord. Do not wait until tomorrow.

> "I may not see
> The rising of the sun.
> When evening falls
> My work all may be done.
> So today is mine —
> Tomorrow may not come."

The Judgments of God

Because Ahab had sold himself to work evil, God said through Elijah that He would bring evil upon him and upon his posterity and cut off all the male members of his household. Concerning Jezebel, God said, "The dogs shall eat Jezebel by the wall of Jezreel. Him that dieth of Ahab in the city the dogs shall eat; and him that dieth in the field shall the fowls of the air eat" (I Kings 21:21-24).

Ahab postponed his own death through partial repentance. We are told that "He rent his clothes, and put sackcloth upon his flesh, and fasted, and lay in sackcloth, and went softly" (I Kings 21:27). Because of this, the Lord said, "I will not bring the evil in his days: but in his son's days will I bring the evil upon his house" (v. 29).

Ahab's death was, nonetheless, a violent death. Some three years later he was severely wounded in battle and died as a result. The record is, "And a certain man drew a bow at a venture, and smote the king of Israel between the joints of the harness: wherefore he said unto the driver of his chariot, Turn thine hand, and carry me out of the host; for I am wounded. And the battle increased that day: and the king . . . died at even: and the blood ran out of the wound into the midst of the chariot. . . . So the King died, and was brought to Samaria, and they buried the king in Samaria. And one washed the chariot in the pool of Samaria; and dogs licked up his blood; and they washed his armour; according unto the word of the Lord which he spake" (I Kings 22:34-38).

It was several years later when divine retribution fell on the head of Jezebel. It took place when Jehu came to Jezreel.

Apparently Jezebel thought that her beauty was sufficient to beguile Jehu so she "painted her face, and tired her head, and looked out at a window" (II Kings 9:30). He would not listen to her and had some of her eunuchs throw her out of her window. "So they threw her down: and some of her blood was sprinkled on the wall, and on the horses: and he trode her under foot" (II Kings 9:33).

After he had eaten the thought occurred to him that after all Jezebel was a king's daughter and ought to be treated with a certain degree of respect, he sent men to bury her, but they found nothing more than the skull and the feet and the palms of her hands. When his servants brought him word, he said, "This is the word of the Lord, which he spake by his servant Elijah the Tishbite, saying, In the portion of Jezreel shall dogs eat the flesh of Jezebel: And the carcase of Jezebel shall be as dung upon the face of the field in the portion of Jezreel; so that they shall not say, This is Jezebel" (II Kings 9:36,37).

This was a fearful judgment, but she was an unrepentant rebel against God. She introduced Baal worship into the palace and into the kingdom in spite of the fact that she had every evidence that God was God. She knew of the miracles performed by Elijah. She reaped what she had sown.

The 10th chapter of II Kings tells how Ahab's family was destroyed: "And it came to pass . . . that they took the king's sons, and slew seventy persons, and put their heads in baskets, and sent him them to Jezreel.

"And there came a messenger, and told him [Jehu], saying, They have brought the heads of the king's sons. And he said, Lay ye them in two heaps at the entering in of the gate until the morning. And it came to pass in the morning, that he went out, and stood, and said to all the people, Ye be righteous: behold, I conspired against my master, and slew him: but who slew all these? Know now that there shall fall unto the earth nothing of the word of the Lord, which the Lord spake concerning the house of Ahab: for the Lord hath done that which he spake by his servant Elijah. So Jehu slew all that remained of the house of Ahab in Jezreel, and all his great men, and his kinsfolks, and his priests, until he left him none remaining" (vv. 7-11).

Just before slaying Jezebel, Jehu had put to death Joram, Ahab's son, who was then king of Israel. Joram had been wounded in a battle with the Syrians and was recuperating from his wounds in Jezreel when Jehu came to the city.

Joram's first words were, "Is it peace, Jehu?" (II Kings 9:22).

He answered, "What peace, so long as the whoredoms of thy mother Jezebel and her witchcrafts are so many?" (v. 22).

At this Joram fled, but Jehu drew a bow, "with his full strength, and smote Jehoram between his arms, and the arrow went out of his heart, and he sunk down in his chariot. Then said Jehu to Bidkar his captain, Take up, and cast him in the portion of the field of Naboth the Jezreelite: for remember how that, when I and thou rode together after Ahab his father, the Lord laid this burden upon him; Surely I have seen yesterday the blood of Naboth, and the blood of his sons, saith the Lord; and I will requite thee in this plat, saith the Lord. Now therefore take and cast him into the plat of ground, according to the word of the Lord" (vv. 24-26). So Joram, the son of Ahab not only met a violent death, but he was buried in the very field his father had murdered Naboth for.

God's judgments are sure. "It is appointed unto men once to die, but after this the judgment" (Heb. 9:27). We cannot get away from it. God said it, and that settles it. Another warning in Hebrews is, "How shall we escape, if we neglect so great salvation" (2:3). This was spoken to those who were already believers, but who did not want to go on to the fullness of the salvation in Christ. Some of us accept salvation from sin's guilt and condemnation but hold back from allowing the living Christ to be our Lord. "How shall we escape, if we neglect so great salvation?"

We considered previously that Ahab showed repentance when Elijah pronounced God's judgment upon him. The king was terror stricken knowing that the words of the prophet would come true. Elijah's word to him was God speaking to him.

Ahab's sin was threefold. First he provoked the anger of God by sinning against Him. Then, not being satisfied that he was provoking God's anger, he made Israel to sin. And in the third place he sold himself to work wickedness.

God's wrath piled up against Ahab as it piles up against sinners of the present day. It is like water piling up in the dam until the pressure is so great that the dam breaks and judgment comes. It will be like that upon the soul that rejects Christ or the chastisement that will come against the believer who wants nothing of the Lordship of Christ.

God's judgment will be severe against men like Ahab who are not satisfied to deny the truth themselves, but lead others down the same corrupt path. Peter warns concerning this in these words: "But there were false prophets also among the people, even as there shall be false teachers among you, who privily shall bring in damnable heresies, even denying the Lord that bought them and bring upon themselves swift destruction" (II Pet. 2:1). There is such preaching in so-called Christian pulpits today and, "Many shall follow their pernicious ways; by reason of whom the way of truth shall be evil spoken of. And through covetousness shall they with feigned words make merchandise of you: whose judgment now of a long time lingereth not, and their damnation [judgment] slumbereth not" (vv. 2,3).

The Lord said there was no one like Ahab who sold himself to work wickedness in the sight of the Lord and who was stirred up by Jezebel his wife. This was an evil combination and showed that Ahab had his price. There is a saying, "Every man has his price." This is not true with regard to the man who is sold out to God.

What price will we sell ourselves for? Will it be material gain? Even some Christians are selling themselves short on salvation in order to gain the riches of this world.

The price for other sinners and God's people alike is the price of honor of profit or pleasure. Ahab sold himself for his affection for Jezebel. However, he was not a man so set in sin that he could not or would not take a warning to heart. When Elijah pronounced judgment upon him, he forgot for a while his pride and his crown and humbled himself. But his repentance was one of fear, not of love. It was not the genuine thing.

In the first place true repentance causes us to view our sins as against God and against God's love. In the second place we see ourselves condemned and guilty and so plead before God. Thirdly, true repentance also reviews the mercies of God which are seen in Christ Jesus His Son. In the fourth place, we accept God's provision of salvation in Christ who died for our sins. Then, in the fifth place, we run from sin as from a serpent, not from the fear of the consequences but because of love for Christ. Finally we present ourselves to God so that He might truly possess us and use us to His own honor and glory. Ahab's repentance was not of this nature. It was fear of the punishment not the sinfulness of sin that caused him to tremble. Had there been no curse placed upon him, his sins and evil ways would have pained him but very little. Yet even this humbling of himself, though it was only partial repentance, brought a stay of judgment. How merciful is our God!

Is He knocking at your heart's door now? If He is, let Him in.

Elijah's Last Task

Before final tragedy overtook the last of Ahab's family an incident recorded in II Kings chapter 1, gives us an insight into the character of Ahab's children and the record of the last public act of the Prophet Elijah.

Following Ahab on the throne was Ahaziah his son. His rule was very brief and his death is an illustration of God's judgment on rebels who persist in defying God. Ahaziah was the playboy type who enjoyed the privileges of rulership, but wanted nothing to do with its harsher realities. Moab rebelled against Israel after the death of Ahab, and Ahaziah could not care less. His attitude was to let Moab rebel. It mattered nothing to him.

This brief bit of history so far as Ahaziah is concerned opens with Ahaziah falling through a lattice work in his upper chamber in Samaria. The fall was apparently severe for he was very ill and wondered if he would recover. He sent messengers with these instructions: "Go, enquire of Baal-zebub the god of Ekron whether I shall recover of this disease" (II Kings 1:2). This god of Ekron was Baal worshipped as the god of medicine by the Philistines and also the god of the flies. This, of course, was the same old demon worship that had brought disaster on Ahab and Israel.

Nothing is hidden from God, and the angel of the Lord "said to Elijah the Tishbite, Arise, go up to meet the messengers of the king of Samaria, and say unto them, Is it not because there is not a God in Israel, that ye go to enquire of Baal-zebub the god of Ekron? Now therefore thus saith the Lord, Thou shalt not come down from that bed upon which thou art gone up, but shalt surely die" (II Kings 1:3,4). Elijah immediately departed with this message. This was the last task God gave him. Just as the prophet had been sent to rebuke Ahab, now he was sent to rebuke Ahab's son.

The messengers turned right around and went back to the king who was surprised to see them so quickly. He said to them: "Why are ye now turned back?" (v. 5).

"And they said unto him, There came a man up to meet us, and said unto us, Go, turn again unto the king that sent you, and say unto him, Thus saith the Lord, Is it not because there is not a God in Israel, that thou sendest to enquire of Baal-zebub the god of Ekron? therefore thou shalt not come down from that bed on which thou art gone up, but shalt surely die" (v. 6).

Ahaziah then asked them: "What manner of man was he which came up to meet you, and told you these words?" (v. 7).

They answered: "He was an hairy man, and girt with a girdle of leather about his loins" (v. 8).

The king immediately identified the man as Elijah the Tishbite. He was not ignorant of the part Elijah had played in the history of Ahab and Israel, but in spite of his knowledge this new king was worse than his father. He sent a captain and 50 soldiers to take Elijah prisoner. This was an open challenge against God himself. Ahaziah was so swollen with personal pride that he thought he could fight against God through fighting God's man.

Do we realize that this will take place again and on a much greater scale? The Battle of Armageddon will be nothing less than the Satan-inspired Antichrist rousing his men, some 200 million of them, to fight against the armies of heaven. They will actually believe they can win in this contest, but they will not. You may mark it that Satan always ends up by sending his stooges to their doom. Some reading these words may even be playing into the hands of the Devil himself. He will not be able to rescue you from the judgment of God. In spite of his fair promises, Satan can guarantee only the wages of sin and that is death.

Evil men will not face the facts of God's judgment. Ahaziah would not and struck out against the person who dared to proclaim God's message. It seems to be a human trait to think that by striking down God's messenger, man also does away with God's judgment. How false this is, for God will not be mocked. A man will reap whatever he sows (Gal. 6:7). God is a consuming fire. It is a fearful thing to fall into His hands in judgment.

When men turn from God's truth as proclaimed in His Word, they are not rejecting so much God's messengers as they are rejecting God himself. Their rebellion is not against men, but against God. They will have to face Him someday and how can they expect to stand in such a judgment?

The soldiers found Elijah on the top of a hill. It might have been Mount Carmel upon which he witnessed God's great triumph in the sending of fire that consumed the offering on the altar. Elijah had gone to this hill, whatever it was, to pray and to fellowship with God. Moses followed this practice and the Lord Jesus did also during the days of his public ministry. The practice speaks of isolation and seclusion, the servant being alone with God.

Judgment by Fire

The captain of the 50 said to Elijah, "Thou man of God, the king hath said, Come down" (II Kings 1:9). The captain may have called Elijah a man of God in mockery, but God cannot be mocked. Elijah sat in safety, for as God's representative he had nothing to fear.

He answered the jibe in these words: "And Elijah answered and said to the captain of the fifty, If I be a man of God, then let fire come down from heaven, and consume thee and thy fifty" (v. 10). God vindicated His servant and fire fell from heaven and consumed the captain and his men.

On Mount Carmel the fire had fallen and consumed the sacrifice while the people went scot-free. The prophets of Baal, of course, were an exception, for they had sold themselves to sin.

On Mount Calvary, God's wrath fell upon His Son who died in our place that we might go free. All God asks is that we accept Christ as our Saviour, trusting Him to save us from sin. But those who refuse, those who will not turn to God will not find the rest God gives His people, but will be judged: "And you who are troubled rest with us, when the Lord Jesus shall be revealed from heaven with his mighty angels, In flaming fire taking vengeance on them that know not [ignore] God, and obey not the gospel of our Lord Jesus Christ: Who shall be punished with everlasting destruction from the presence of the Lord, and from the glory of his power" (II Thess. 1:7-9).

These soldiers came without repentant hearts and without a sacrifice and so faced the judgment of their own sin. They did not turn to God. The warning in the Scripture is: "Without shedding of blood is no remission [of sin]" (Heb. 9:22). The Bible also warns: "It is a fearful thing to fall into the hands of the living God."

Elijah's calling down fire upon these men was not the result of personal revenge on his part. He was a true servant of God and reflected the heart of God who finds no pleasure in the death of the wicked. God is ". . . longsuffering to us-ward, not willing that any should perish, but that all should come to repentance" (II Pet. 3:9).

The king learned nothing from the loss of these men and sent out a second captain with 50 soldiers. Perhaps Ahaziah and some of the others thought that an accident had taken place. They may have thought the death of these men was caused by lightning and was not the result of God's direct judgment. But they ignored the evidence which was startling and clear. The bodies of the slain men were mute testimony to what had taken place. Elijah answered this second captain as he had the first and fire came down from heaven and consumed them (II Kings 1:12).

One wonders how blind and calloused a man can become. Ahaziah had sent over a hundred men to their death, yet he sent a third group with the same instructions — to bring Elijah in.

The captain of this third 50 was different than the others. He "came and fell on his knees before Elijah, and besought him, and said unto him, O man of God, I pray thee, let my life, and the life of these fifty thy servants, be precious in thy sight. Behold, there came fire down from heaven, and burnt up the two captains of the former fifties with their fifties: therefore let my life be now precious in thy sight" (vv. 13,14).

This captain approached God's servant showing reverence in his heart for God and pleaded for mercy. He showed submission to the living God. This must have caused Elijah to rejoice, for, like God, he had no pleasure in the death of the wicked. Nevertheless judgment has been sent by God on several occasions to warn the ungodly: "For if God spared not the angels that sinned, but cast them down to hell, and delivered them into chains of darkness, to be reserved unto judgment; And spared not the old world, but saved Noah the eighth person, a preacher of righteousness, bringing in the flood upon the world of the ungodly; And turning the cities of Sodom and Gomorrha into ashes condemned them with an overthrow, making them an ensample unto those that after should live ungodly" (II Pet. 2:4-6).

Elijah was assured by the angel of the Lord that no harm would come to him and that he was to go down with the captain and give God's message to the king in person. Soon after this Ahaziah died and Jehoram reigned in his place.

All men who reject Jesus Christ will meet Him in person: "And I saw a great white throne, and him that sat on it, from whose face the earth and the heaven fled away; and there was found no place for them. And I saw the dead, small and great, stand before God; and the books were opened: and another book was opened, which is the book of life: and the dead were judged out of those things which were written in the books, according to their works. And the sea gave up the dead which were in it; and death and hell delivered up the dead which were in them: and they were judged every man according to their works. And death and hell were cast into the lake of fire. This is the second death. And whosoever was not found written in the book of life was cast into the lake of fire" (Rev. 20:11-15).

"Prepare to meet thy God."

CHAPTER THIRTEEN

THE TRANSLATION OF ELIJAH

The closing incident in Elijah's life was perhaps the most touching in his whole history. He was translated to heaven without having to die. His ministry may have covered 15 or 20 years, but the public aspect of it was much briefer than that. At a time of great depression in his life, when lying under a juniper tree, he had prayed for death, but when the time of his translation came he would be thankful that God had not answered that prayer.

The prophet's translation was to be at a specially designated place. Elijah had learned long before this that absolute obedience to God's directions was necessary for God's blessings. Only at the Brook Cherith were the ravens instructed to bring food to him. Only in the city of Zarephath was there a widow with a little oil and meal who would sustain him. So Elijah knew how essential it was to be in the right place in order to see the fulfillment of God's promises.

The record of this great event is found in II Kings 2. In verse 1 we are told that when the Lord would take up Elijah into heaven by a whirlwind the prophet with his servant Elisha took his journey by first leaving Gilgal. In his retiring years he had been training young men, possibly some of the 7000 who had not bowed their knee to Baal. He had established three schools, one in Gilgal, one at Beth-el, and one in Jericho. This was not a new thing in Israel; Samuel had done this long before. Young prophets came out of these schools who were used of the Lord, men like Amos.

Elijah began his journey from Gilgal to the place of his ascension, and Elisha insisted in going with him. This journey involved a great test for Elisha who was to be Elijah's successor.

167

From the account one may be led to think that Elijah was reluctant to have Elisha go with him, but this may well have been part of the test for the younger man. Elijah was a man who was much alone in his ministry, and he was a humble man, and he may have felt that his coming translation was too sacred a matter to be witnessed by others.

There are valuable lessons for us to learn from this experience. If we wish to behold the glory of God and to be fit vessels to participate in God's work so as to proclaim and demonstrate something of that glory, we must go on to the realities of a deeper experience with Christ.

Gilgal

As we have already seen, Elijah's journey began at Gilgal. This place is noteworthy, not only because one of Elijah's schools was there, but it marked Israel's first beachhead when they came into the land of promise. It was their home base for all their operations during the first four or five years of their campaign to take over Canaan. They returned again and again to this spot for meditation on the Word of God and to receive strength from the Lord. This was the place they received their instructions for their day-by-day living. It speaks to us of the comforts of Christianity, the home base, where things are safe and secure for us.

If we go no farther than this in our experience as believers, however, we will show lack of vision and lack of determination with regard to great and vital decisions in our lives. This was the first test that came to Elisha when he made it known he wanted to follow Elijah.

Verse 2 of this chapter says: "And Elijah said unto Elisha, Tarry here [at Gilgal], I pray thee; for the Lord hath sent me to Beth-el. And Elisha said unto him, As the Lord liveth, and as thy soul liveth, I will not leave thee. So they went down to Beth-el."

Elisha was given the opportunity to stay at Gilgal, which represents the easy place for Christian living. It is not so hard to be a Christian, to be born again, to attend a good Bible-believing church with its regular services on a Sunday, and possibly a prayer meeting during the week. Added to this would be private, personal devotions which is also beneficial and essential to the Christian life. This is all good and we may be little bothered in such a situation except by the Devil or the flesh. Here there is no call for any vital decisions. There is little or no participation in spiritual warfare. We go along from day to day anticipating that the Lord will one day call us home to heaven rejoicing.

Beth-el

Beth-el speaks of something else again. The word itself means "house of God." This was where Jacob first met God when he fled from Esau. It was the place to which God called Jacob back after he had been with Laban for 20 years. It was the place of major decisions in Jacob's life, and he should have stayed closer to it.

Beth-el speaks to us of a once-for-all decision that we as believers must make. The New Testament places this before us in these words: "I beseech you therefore, brethren, by the mercies of God, that ye present your bodies a living sacrifice, holy, acceptable unto God, which is your reasonable service" (Rom. 12:1). There comes a time in our Christian experience when we each have to face this decision.

We need to analyze this verse very carefully. It comes at a place in the Book of Romans following the portion in which God has definitely outlined the marvelous plan for the Christian's life. It is to be a life of complete victory, a life of usefulness to God. Before this can be realized God must have complete possession of us. This is seen in the phrase "present [yield] your bodies a living sacrifice." The Lord has purchased this body for His own possession (I Cor. 6:19). We are not our own any more; nevertheless, He does not force Himself upon us. He indwells us when we are born again, but He may only be given the guest room in our hearts. He needs all of us, however, in order to live His life in us through Christ Jesus our Lord.

This is to be a once-for-all decision in yielding our bodies to God for living sacrifices. The word "sacrifice" itself speaks of death and yet this is to be a living sacrifice which speaks of activity. This seeming paradox is explained in the fact that we are to die to self but to be alive unto God through an act of faith. This is taught in Romans 6:11 and is our reasonable service. Nothing is to be held back. Beth-el speaks to us of this great choice.

Elijah said the Lord had sent him from Gilgal to Beth-el. His had been a life of direct orders from God and explicit obedience to those orders. How would Elisha measure up in these things? That was the test, but there was no hesitancy with Elisha. The expression "as the Lord liveth, and as thy soul liveth, I will not leave thee" may be restated thus: "As sure as God lives in you and in me I will not leave you." This is an absolute and final statement. This is a choice from which there is no backing down.

This was a willing decision that Elisha made, and it is the kind of decision God requires of us. He never forces Himself upon us. Once we make this decision in God's favor there is no limit to what He can do through us. When we give our bodies over to Him completely we find we can say, as did Paul: "I can do all things through Christ which strengtheneth me" (Phil. 4:13).

Stating it from another angle, Paul said in Galatians 2:20, the last part of the verse: "The life which I now live in the flesh I live by the faith of the Son of God, who loved me, and gave himself for me."

Recognizing then that there must be a complete surrender on our part, let us not stop at Gilgal, which represents ease of Christian living, but let us go on to Beth-el, where He calls upon us for a full surrender to Him. He does not ask us all to be preachers or missionaries or full-time personal workers, but He does ask us to present our bodies so that He may indwell us completely in every aspect of our being.

Jericho

In the 4th verse of II Kings 2, we read: "And Elijah said unto him, Elisha, tarry here, I pray thee; for the Lord hath sent me to Jericho." Elijah said in effect to Elisha that since he had made his decision to go along with the Lord, he would not be stopping short to stay there at Beth-el. He had come a long way in the Christian life (looking at it from the standpoint of the application we have been making), so he could afford to stay for a while at Beth-el.

But this was not Elisha's decision. Again he said, "As the Lord liveth, and as thy soul liveth, I will not leave thee. So they came to Jericho" (v. 4).

Jericho represents the place of spiritual warfare, entering into activity against forces of evil in the heavenlies for the Lord. This goes far beyond the average Christian's church-going, attending evangelistic campaigns—all of which is good —but this goes much farther. This is the hardest phase of Christian living, but one we must enter into if we would reap the greatest benefits in service and rewards. This is not something that is done in public, but in private. There is no glamour to this side of the Christian life, but it makes for effective service when entered into in the power of the Lord.

Three Steps in Israel's Deliverance

Looking at the three basic steps in Israel's deliverance from Egypt will help us see what is involved in this truth. First of all, when the Israelites were slaves in Egypt they could do nothing to help themselves. God had to liberate them and He did. The blood on the doorposts of the houses was the sign of their salvation. The manifestation of God's power at the Red Sea which delivered them completely from Egypt and its armies speaks of the moving out of death into life which is in God himself. This was all God's doing. It represents what in our lives is our deliverance from the guilt and condemnation of sin and emancipation from the world. But what follows?

The second great experience for Israel was in the desert. It was there they were to learn to follow God completely so that they would be separated not only from a sinful world but from a sinful self-life. One generation never did learn this, for all they did was murmur. They went in circles, wandering in the desert for some 40 years. This is true of a lot of believers who settle down in mere church life. They fail to go on to complete consecration and separation to the Lord and to enter into spiritual warfare. They follow a program of church attendance week-in and week-out, but they make no progress in their Christian lives because they have no purpose beyond attending meetings. This is no better than Israel's wandering in the wilderness and murmuring and traveling in circles. To do the former is right, but to fail to grow in the Christian life is sin. "That which is not of faith is sin."

The third great experience for Israel came when they crossed the Jordan. Then it was they came to Jericho and entered into warfare in order to possess the land. They were useless to God so far as their testimony was concerned while in Egypt and in the desert. It was not until they came to the land itself that God could work through them to possess it.

We are useless to God as long as we are in the world. We are useless to Him also as long as we merely follow a church program and play church instead of getting out of the self-life and into the full life of separation and warfare represented by Canaan.

As soon as Israel entered the promised land Satanic opposition appeared. We can expect this also as soon as we enter into spiritual warfare. That is why Ephesians 6 was written. "Finally, my brethren, be strong in the Lord, and in the power of his might. Put on the whole armour of God, that ye may be able to stand against the wiles of the devil. For we wrestle not against flesh and blood, but against principalities, against powers, against the rulers of the darkness of this world, against spiritual wickedness in high places. Wherefore take unto you the whole armour of God, that ye may be able to withstand in the evil day, and having done all, to stand" (Eph. 6:10-13).

In this spiritual warfare God provides armor for our protection where necessary and for offensive battle He furnishes us with the sword. Through faith we enter into this active service with Him which is climaxed by warfare through prayer. God needs more prayer warriors today among His people. Let us join this aggressive group.

Jordan

Elisha chose to go with Elijah to Jericho just as he had chosen to go with him to Beth-el. But now their journey took them even farther. Elijah asked Elisha to stay at Jericho for, said he, "The Lord hath sent me to Jordan" (v. 6). Again Elisha refused and journeyed with his master. Jordan speaks of death. It represents death to the self-life. Jordan stands as the place of Israel's separation from the self-life in the desert to the life of warfare for the Lord in the land.

Have we passed through this in our daily experience? True, we have been born again, and have been united to Christ. We have been identified with Him in His death and burial and resurrection. But not until we appropriate this by faith and enter into it actively in His Name does it mean anything to us.

The cardinal chapter of the Bible for this subject is Romans 6. There we read: "Knowing this that our old man is crucified with him, that the body of sin might be destroyed, that henceforth we should not serve sin" (v. 6). This speaks of the potential of the Christian life. But in order actually to enter into it, here is what is needed: "Likewise reckon ye also yourselves [this is by an act of faith] to be dead indeed unto sin, but alive unto God through Jesus Christ our Lord" (Rom. 6:11). We are to count this true in our lives.

All four of the gospel writers have something to say on this subject. In Matthew 10:38,39 we read, "And he that taketh not his cross [this speaks of this death], and followeth after me, is not worthy of me. He that findeth his life shall lose it [speaking of trying to find our own way in this earthly life]: and he that loseth his life for my sake shall find it." If we are willing to give up our self-life for His sake we really begin to live.

In Mark 8:34 we learn: "And when he had called the people unto him with his disciples also, he said unto them, Whosoever will come after me, let him deny himself, and take up his cross, and follow me. . . . Whosoever shall be ashamed of me and of my words in this adulterous and sinful generation; of him also shall the Son of man be ashamed, when he cometh in the glory of his Father with the holy angels."

Paul provides a practical demonstration of this. When told by friends that if he went to Jerusalem he would be made a prisoner and possibly put to death, he said: "But none of

these things move me, neither count I my life dear unto myself, so that I might finish my course with joy, and the ministry,
which I have received of the Lord Jesus, to testify the gospel of
the grace of God." He was willing to lay down his life if it would
mean the accomplishing of the ministry which God had entrusted him with. His self-life had no value to him. This was
Elisha's attitude also when he followed Elijah to the Jordan
and beyond.

A very important decision must be made by all of us. Our
Lord said in Luke 14:26,27: "If any man come to me, and hate
not his father, and mother, and wife, and children, and
brethren, and sisters, yea, and his own life also, he cannot be
my disciple. And whosoever doth not bear his cross, and come
after me, cannot be my disciple." We may be children of God
but we cannot be disciples in the sense of one who is learning
and serving unless we put God in first place ahead of all earthly ties or ambitions.

In John's Gospel our Lord said, "I say unto you, Except a
corn of wheat fall into the ground and die, it abideth alone: but
if it die, it bringeth forth much fruit" (12:24).

Along this same line, and pressing on us for a decision,
are our Lord's words in Luke 14:33: "So likewise, whosoever
he be of you that forsaketh not all that he hath, he cannot be
my disciple." This is why Paul said in Philippians 3 that he
counted all the personal and early religious accomplishments
of life as loss for Christ: "I count all things but loss for the
excellency of the knowledge of Christ Jesus my Lord." Is Christ
our Lord? If so, we will not hesitate to go on with Him.

Turning back again to the story of Elijah and Elisha, we
learn in II Kings 2:7,8: "And fifty men of the sons of the
prophets went, and stood to view afar off: and they two [Elijah
and Elisha] stood by Jordan. And Elijah took his mantle, and
wrapped it together, and smote the waters, and they were
divided hither and thither, so that they two went over on dry
ground." This was an act of faith on Elijah's part. God held
back the waters of the Jordan River because of this expression
of faith and His two servants committed themselves to Him.

They did not ask how God held back the waters but trusted Him to do it.

The cross life, concerning which we have been commenting, is a faith life. We accept by faith our death in Christ. We do not understand this necessarily, but we accept it by faith and we find that it works. When we believe God in these matters He takes over. The Christian life is a life of faith and every step is a step of faith. Faith cometh by hearing and hearing by the Word of God. Thus the life of faith is the life of obedience to God's revealed Word.

The Principle of Faith

Elijah did not stand on the banks of the river waiting for God to do something. Faith, true faith results in action. The river had to part and Elijah struck it with his mantle. God had parted the river for Joshua and the Israelites long before this, so that this particular miracle was not new. What God did once, surely He would do again. The waters parted as Elijah desired.

There was faith in operation as He and Elisha walked through the bed of the river. The water coming down from above suddenly stopped as though someone had built a dam. There was no dam visible just as the hand of God is not visible. Water that had already passed continued to recede and soon the two men were able to cross on dry ground.

While they were passing through the bed of the river, they very possibly saw the water being piled up as the river continued to flow above them. How could they be sure that this body of water would not suddenly give way and they be drowned? This was where faith entered in again. There was not only faith in the parting of the water, but faith was in evidence also in their passing through the bed of the river. This shows that we must by faith appropriate what God has done for us. We must accept it as a fact and venture out on the basis of it. It is not merely a matter of saying, "Lord I believe that you can deliver me from sin and its enslavement." Faith without works is a dead faith. We must act upon it as did these two men in crossing the Jordan.

In these several steps in which we have been following
Elisha as he journeyed with Elijah, we have seen each was a
matter of believing. It raises this question, "How do I know
that I am separated unto God? Does the reality of my separation depend on how earnest I was at the time I surrendered my
life?" Not necessarily. Earnestness has its part, but the essential was the believing or the faith when we said "yes" to
God. We place ourselves in His hands, and He does the separat-
ing. This sanctification or separation is a matter of God's doing.
He separates us to Himself.

Then what about the matter of entering into spiritual
warfare? How do I know that God will answer my prayer and
accept my decision? We believe that God will do this because
He has said so. We step out in faith, and this applies to every
aspect of our Christian life. Only as God sees us moving forward will He be able to work on our behalf. We must by faith
move forward with Him.

This is a lesson the Lord taught us personally many years
ago. The very incident of Israel crossing the Jordan River was
the Scripture the Lord used to bring forceably to our hearts
and minds that He wanted us to step out by faith. This was
over a quarter of a century ago when God brought us to Lincoln, Nebraska, to begin the Back to the Bible Broadcast. We
had to step out in faith, burning all bridges behind us. We
trusted only in God for there was no visible means of support
from any other source.

It has been the same principle of faith that we have sought
to follow all through the years since then. We sign contracts
with stations, not waiting until there is money on hand.
When we believe God has allowed us to go ahead, we do so.
We undertake missionary work by faith and God has met
the needs.

Elisha's Request

After Elijah and Elisha had crossed the river, Elijah said
to the younger man: "Ask what I shall do for thee, before I be
taken from thee. And Elisha said, I pray thee, let a double
portion of thy spirit be upon me" (II Kings 2:9).

In this there is an unlimited potential. Elisha was first to ask what he wanted Elijah to do for him. This threw the gate wide open, so to speak, to this young man. This brings force-ably before us what God will do for us, for Elijah could do for Elisha only what God would give. Our Saviour said, in Luke 11:13: "If ye then, being evil, know how to give good gifts unto your children: how much more shall your heavenly Father give the Holy Spirit to them that ask him?" How many persons responded ahead of Pentecost to this promise? Another great promise is found in Matthew 7:7,8: "Ask, and it shall be given you; seek, and ye shall find; knock, and it shall be opened unto you: For every one that asketh receiveth; and he that seeketh findeth; and to him that knocketh it shall be opened." If we do not receive from God, it is because we have not asked Him according to James 4:2.

Let us not blame God if we do not see in our lives what we think ought to be there. We have either not surrendered our lives to the Lord; or we have not accepted by faith what God has already accomplished for us in Christ Jesus; or we simply have not asked.

On this particular occasion, Elisha showed what was deep in his own heart. His answer is something for us to ponder, as we think of what the goal in our life might be. Is it success of some kind? Is it something that God can honor?

The various testings Elisha had passed through from Gilgal to the time when he was asked what Elijah could do for him, were stepping-stones of faith. They led up to that great climax. Elisha's answer was, "I pray thee, let a double portion of thy spirit be upon me."

This was in the spirit of Paul's aspiration when he declared that he had left all things behind him in order that he might attain to the excellency of the knowledge of Christ Jesus. He wanted to know Christ and the power of His resurrection and the fellowship of His sufferings, "Being made conformable unto his death" that he might experience daily the resurrection life of Christ in him. He did not feel that he had already attained, but he followed after and pressed toward the mark of the prize of the high calling of God in Christ Jesus.

The question that was put to Elisha is not something that can be put to just anybody, for not all are ready for it. But this verse in the Psalms is the key to receiving from God the best things: "Delight thyself also in the Lord; and he shall give thee the desires of thine heart" (Ps. 37:4).

This is a verse that I have meditated on for many, many years and though I have experienced it in part, I am still conscious of failure to always delight myself in the Lord.

When our goal in life is to do the will of God, He will open our eyes to see what we should desire and make our purpose in life.

Paul's prayer for the Ephesians and for us is: "That the God of our Lord Jesus Christ, the Father of glory, may give unto you the spirit of wisdom and revelation in the knowledge of him: The eyes of your understanding being enlightened; that ye may know what is the hope of his calling, and what the riches of the glory of his inheritance in the saints" (1:17,18).

There was an unlimited potential before Elisha and he wasted no time in making known his God-given desire.

Elisha Given Elijah's Mantle

Elisha had sat at the feet of Elijah for some ten years. He had seen what it meant to be a servant of God, to have a surrendered heart and a holy life. He also witnessed how God honors such a person. For his own part, Elisha was totally consecrated to the Lord. He had passed many tests from the day that Elijah had cast his mantle on him; and in the events leading up to the crossing of the Jordan, he had again proved that he wanted to go all the way with the Lord.

The casting of the mantle upon him was significant. In Jewish customs it was the sign of adoption as a son. In Elisha's case it meant that he was adopted by Elijah to be a spiritual heir of the prophet. Just as the first-born in Israel had the right to a double portion of the inheritance, so Elisha in asking for a double portion of the Spirit that rested upon Elijah was being consistent with the position he held. He was not necessarily the first individual Elijah had led into a true worship of the Lord, but he was picked out to be the spiritual son and successor of this prophet of God.

Elisha did not ask for more of the Holy Spirit. A person either receives the Holy Spirit or does not. A true believer always does receive Him. The question we need to ponder is how much does the Holy Spirit have of us.

In asking for a double portion of the Spirit, Elisha had reference to the ministry he was to inherit. In regard to this it is no accident that he had twice as many miracles recorded to his credit as did Elijah, and he ministered twice as long as Elijah. This was not something that was done without absolute surrender on his part to the Spirit of God. Such a ministry cannot be fulfilled on the human level. It is a divine work in the first place and must be energized by God.

Elijah's answer is given in verse 10: "And he said, Thou hast asked a hard thing: nevertheless, if thou see me when I am taken from thee, it shall be so unto thee; but if not, it shall not be so." This was not something Elijah himself could promise, for it was not his prerogative to give. With his prophetic insight, however, he could say to Elisha, "If I am carried away in full view of thee, then the request is granted; if not, it is refused." This was the same as saying that if Elisha saw Elijah being translated, then he should accept it as a sign from God that his request had been granted.

There was a spiritual factor to this translation of Elijah. Only a man whose spiritual qualities were right before God would be permitted to view this actual scene. Just as there are sounds beyond the hearing of the human ear, just so are there realities that the human eye cannot see. The chariot of fire and the horses of fire were real though not all who were watching Elijah and Elisha saw them. The Bible tells us that God has appointed angels as guardians of His people and part of His care for us is through them. Little children have their guardian angels, according to the Scriptures, but none of these are visible to our human sight.

Fifty young prophets stood by the river watching, but they did not see what Elisha saw. The Spirit of God did not give them the spiritual insight and endowment because they were not prepared for it Elijah had passed the test of Beth-el which speaks of separation, the test of Jericho which speaks of warfare, and the test of Jordan which speaks of death and resurrection. These others had not.

In the sixth chapter of II Kings is a very good illustration of this whole matter. Elisha was established as God's prophet, and being God's man was, of course, the target for God's enemies. Ben-hadad, king of Syria, made war on Israel but found that the secret plans that he talked of in his private chambers were known almost immediately to the king of Israel. The Syrian king learned that Elisha, the prophet, was informing the Israelites of his plans, and so he determined to capture him.

Soon after, he sent an army to surround the city of Dothan with the hope of taking Elisha. The prophet's servant discovered this when he arose early one morning and found a host with horses and chariots encircling the town. He ran to his master terrified.

Elisha said to him, "Fear not: for they that be with us are more than they that be with them" (II Kings 6:16). Then Elisha prayed a remarkable prayer and said, "Lord, I pray thee, open his eyes, that he may see. And the Lord opened the eyes of the young man; and he saw: and, behold, the mountain was full of horses and chariots of fire round about Elisha" (v. 17). It took a special manifestation of God's power for this young man to see what was a reality with regard to spiritual forces around the city of Dothan. This was the kind of thing that Elijah said if it happened to Elisha he could take it as an assurance that his request was pleasing to God.

Paul's prayer for the Ephesians and for us is not that our physical eyes shall see things that ordinarily they cannot see, but that our spiritual vision shall be clarified to where our faith will lay hold of God's promises. Paul prayed for "the spirit of wisdom and revelation in the knowledge of him: The eyes of your understanding being enlightened; that ye may know what is the hope of his calling, and what the riches of the glory of his inheritance in the saints" (Eph. 1:17,18).

Elisha did see this great event, for we learn: "And it came

to pass, as they still went on, and talked, that, behold, there appeared a chariot of fire, and horses of fire, and parted them both asunder; and Elijah went up by a whirlwind into heaven" (II Kings 2:11).

His great request was answered!

CHAPTER FOURTEEN

ELISHA ACCEPTS ELIJAH'S UNFINISHED TASK

The horses of fire and the chariots of fire speak of Elijah's fiery message. He was a prophet of fire. And he came and went like a whirlwind. It surely is quite significant that this is the closing scene of Elijah's earthly ministry.

It was also, of course, the beginning of Elisha's own ministry as he carried the responsibilities laid down by his former teacher. This is one reason why he cried: "My father, my father, the chariot of Israel, and the horsemen thereof. And he saw him no more: and he took hold of his own clothes, and rent them in two pieces" (II Kings 2:12). As the weight of this new responsibility began to break on Elisha's mind and heart it broke his heart, and he saw that in himself he could not carry it through.

Elijah had been like a father to him. Now the older prophet was gone and this left Elisha in the forefront of the battle.

I personally have some understanding of this situation. On the 22nd day of December, 1945, I stood in a mortuary in Kansas looking upon the face of the man who had meant more to me than any other person on earth — my own father. Several friends and relatives were standing by when I found myself overcome by emotion and wept. Mother came over to me and patted me on the shoulder and said, "Now son, now son." I said to her that it was not because Dad was taken that I was weeping, though I would miss his fellowship, but it was the sudden realization that many responsibilities that had been on his shoulders were now transferred to mine. I could no longer

183

go to him and ask him questions or pray with him or counsel with him. It was the realization of this overwhelming responsibility that upset me emotionally.

Elijah through his ministry and his prayer life had been a protector of Israel. This is why Elisha cried, "The chariot of Israel, and the horsemen thereof." Moses did the same for Israel in his day as he interceded for them before God.

The rending of his garments indicated Elisha's recognition of his own inability and his insufficiency. It spoke of his brokenness before God and his appeal to God for His divine strength.

I heard a sermon once by a dear brother who came to pastor a church that had been ministered to for more than one generation by a dearly-loved man of God. This former pastor had been one of God's great stalwart soldiers, a spiritual giant in many ways. For a new man to pick up where this former pastor had left off was a difficult assignment. There were people there along in years who had known only one pastor in 40 years. He meant everything to them, and it was natural that they would gauge a new preacher by the pattern set by the one who had gone on to be with the Lord.

The sermon I heard from the incoming pastor was one of the finest on this subject that I have ever heard. It was from the first chapter of Joshua concerning that portion where the Lord said to Joshua, "Moses, my servant, is dead." The man who had been Joshua's leader and Israel's leader for 40 years was gone. This, however, was not all that God had to say. He continued: "Now therefore arise, go over this Jordan, thou, and all this people, unto the land which I do give to them, even to the children of Israel. Every place that the sole of your foot shall tread upon, that have I given unto you, as I said unto Moses. From the wilderness and this Lebanon even unto the great river, the river Euphrates, all the land of the Hittites, and unto the great sea toward the going down of the sun, shall be your coast. There shall not any man be able to stand before thee all the days of thy life: as I was with Moses, so I will be with thee: I will not fail thee, nor forsake thee. Be strong and of a good courage . . ." (Josh. 1:2-6).

This pastor went on to say, "I realize that many of you wonder if I can fill the shoes of your former pastor. I can never do that. I did not come here to fill his shoes. I would have had to turn down this invitation to pastor this flock if it were not for the consolation that I have from this message from God to Joshua when he said, 'As I was with Moses, so will I be with thee!' "

Elijah was gone, but God was still present. God is the ever-living One, and though His servants are removed from this earthly scene He continues, for His years never fail. This was what gave Elisha the courage to accept the challenge even though he did it with a broken heart. His acceptance is demonstrated through his picking up the mantle of Elijah. "He took up also the mantle of Elijah that fell from him, and went back, and stood by the bank of Jordan" (II Kings 2:13). This garment was a loose cloak thrown about the shoulders and had become the recognized dress of the prophets of Jehovah. Elisha entered into that office accepting the gift of prophecy by faith.

Picking up Elijah's mantle meant that Elisha would stand with God just as the older prophet had done. That he would be able to do so he had the assurance in that he had seen Elijah's translation, and the prophet's garment had been left behind for him.

Recrossing the Jordan

Elisha returned to the Jordan and "took the mantle of Elijah that fell from him, and smote the waters, and said, Where is the Lord God of Elijah? and when he also had smitten the waters, they parted hither and thither: and Elisha went over" (II Kings 2:14). The Lord made it possible for Elisha to cross the Jordan dry-shod just as He had done for Elijah. He was gone, but his God remained.

It is very possible that Elisha did not feel any different when he found himself endued with power from above. There is no record that he went through a great emotional experience; nevertheless, he had come to a place where an act of faith was needed, and he acted. There was no doubting of God in this action of Elisha's. Rather it was an act of confidence because he believed that God who had given Elijah power was now empowering him.

Some 3000 years have gone by since those days. Has God died? Has He lost power? Is the lack of faith so evident in many quarters today due to God's failure, or our deterioration in spiritual things? This is an age when we are inclined to be dazzled by the inventions of men, but God is the same God now as He was in Elijah and Elisha's time. His power has not diminished. The question is, "Have we made this God our God?" Men are looking for better methods and God is looking for better men. There was a time when He looked for a man and did not find one (Ezek. 22:30), but in Elijah's day and Elisha's day, these were the men He found to do His work.

There was still another reason why God demonstrated His power for Elisha in parting the waters of Jordan. The sons of the prophets had watched what they could see of the parting of these two men. At least Elijah's mantle would be visible to them and the fact that Elisha picked it up and then the fact that he smote the waters of Jordan and they parted. For we read: "When the sons of the prophets which were to view at Jericho saw him, they said, The spirit of Elijah doth rest on Elisha. And they came to meet him, and bowed themselves to the ground before him" (v. 15). There was a revival among them when they saw the power of God upon the new leader.

God is still able to bring revival today, and He will when He finds hearts responding to Him and submitting themselves completely to His leading and direction. Revival is not necessarily prayed down. It is brought down when we believe God and trust Him.

Elisha's Fourfold Heritage From Elijah

There is no use in studying the Bible if we do not apply its truths to our lives. This is what we mean by meditating on the Word. We look into the Word of God which serves as a mirror and reveals our lives, then we turn to God and ask Him to cleanse us and to change us to His glory. The Psalmist said, "Thy word have I hid in mine heart, that I might not sin against thee." Bible truth will mean nothing to us unless we make the application of it to our lives.

Elijah's Mantle

The first heritage received by Elisha was the mantle of his master. When Elijah cast it off he threw off forever the burden of his earthly ministry and commission. It is true that according to prophecy he will again appear on the earthly scene but that task will not have anything to do with his ministry of some 3000 years ago. The commission laid down by Elijah was part of the heritage he decreed to Elisha so the work begun by the older prophet would be carried on to its consummation.

This was symbolically presented in the mantle which Elijah dropped and which the Lord carried to Elisha. The younger man accepted it, but it would have been of little significance had not God's power gone along with it. God's work, though it is done by men, must be done in His wisdom and strength.

There is an important lesson in this for us. Suppose Elisha had said, "No, I won't have anything to do with this mantle," meaning that he would not have anything to do with carrying on the work that Elijah had left. This would have been a serious breakdown in the relaying of God's work from one servant to another. The Lord Jesus tells us in John 15:16: "Ye have not chosen me, but I have chosen you, and ordained you, that ye should go and bring forth fruit, and that your fruit should remain." Here we have the evidence that we are to carry on the message begun by our Lord, and that we are divinely commissioned to do so.

In Acts chapter 1, we have the record of our Saviour's last meeting with His disciples before His ascension from the Mount of Olives. Here is what we read: "And, being assembled together with them, commanded them that they should not depart from Jerusalem, but wait for the promise of the Father, which, saith he, ye have heard of me. For John truly baptized with water; but ye shall be baptized with the Holy Ghost not many days hence" (Acts 1:4,5). The disciples were not to leave

Jerusalem until they had witnessed the coming of the Holy Spirit. They were concerned about the coming of the kingdom, but the Lord reminded them that the kingdom was not a subject they needed to be taken up with at that time.

Their great need was to wait as He had commanded, for He said, "Ye shall receive power, after that the Holy Ghost is come upon you: and ye shall be witnesses unto me both in Jerusalem, and in all Judaea, and in Samaria, and unto the uttermost part of the earth. And when he had spoken these things, while they beheld, he was taken up; and a cloud received him out of their sight" (vv. 8,9). The same truth is approached from another angle by the Apostle Paul in II Corinthians 5:18: "And all things are of God, who hath reconciled us to himself by Jesus Christ, and hath given to us the ministry of reconciliation." In the next two verses he tells us what that message is that we are to give to others: "To wit, that God was in Christ, reconciling the world unto himself, not imputing their trespasses unto them; and hath committed unto us the word of reconciliation. Now then we are ambassadors for Christ, as though God did beseech you by us: we pray you in Christ's stead, be ye reconciled to God" (vv. 19,20).

We, then, like Elisha, have been commissioned to finish a task begun by another. We have been chosen of God for this purpose as was Elisha. But just as he could not do the work in his own power — and God did not expect him to — neither can we carry on in our own strength. It is after the coming of the Holy Spirit to give God's people power that they will be able to witness for Him according to Acts 1:8.

God calls us to absolute surrender of ourselves, so that His work through us will be done as He planned it should be done. We are to glorify God in our body and in our spirit which are God's (I Cor. 6:19).

We will be called upon at the Judgment Seat of Christ to answer for what we have done with the heritage received from our Lord. This was of great concern to Paul, for He said, "Wherefore we labour, that, whether present or absent, we may be accepted [pleasing] of him. For we must all appear before the judgment seat of Christ; that every one may receive the things done in his body, according to that he hath done, whether it be good or bad" (II Cor. 5:9,10). Elisha received a call from heaven to go and do God's work. We, too, have received such a call to complete the work our Saviour began.

Elijah's God

The second part of the heritage was that Elijah's God remained with Elisha. There was not only the mantle which spoke of the call to the work, but he had the assurance that the God who wrought miracles through Elijah was also with him to do the same. This is why he said as he smote the waters of Jordan: "Where is the Lord God of Elijah?" (II Kings 2:14).

The mantle would have been an empty thing if the God of Elijah had not proven himself to be on the side of Elisha.

We not only have been called to work for the Lord, but we also have the assurance of His presence with us. Not only did our Lord say, "Go ye into all the world, and preach the gospel" (Mark 16:15), but He also said, "And, lo, I am with you alway" (Matt. 28:20). We direct our prayers to the Father through the Son. We can ask, "Where is the God and Father of our Lord Jesus Christ?" in the same sense Elisha asked, "Where is the Lord God of Elijah?"

The presence of God with us is deeper and fuller than we often think, for the Lord's prayer in John 17 is for our oneness with Him and the Father. "That they all may be one; as thou, Father, art in me, and I in thee, that they also may be one in us: that the world may believe that thou hast sent me" (John 17:21). And then in verse 23 of the same chapter of John, our Saviour said, "I in them, and thou in me, that they may be made perfect in one; and that the world may know that thou hast sent me, and hast loved them, as thou hast loved me."

Previous to this time our Lord had said, "If a man love me, he will keep my words: and my Father will love him, and we will come unto him, and make our abode with him" (John 14:23). There need be no question, then, with regard to the fact that God is with us. He not only has sent us out to be His ambassadors, but we have the firm assurance of His indwelling presence.

Elijah's Spirit

When the waters parted for Elisha at the Jordan River, there was the witness that the Spirit of God was upon him (II Kings 2:14). The same Spirit that energized Elijah energized Elisha. Without the power and the presence of the Holy Spirit Elisha's ministry would have been impossible.

Elisha may not have felt a bit different when he inherited the Spirit's presence and fullness in his life, but he accepted it as a fact by faith. This is something we must do also.

In writing to the Ephesians, Paul said, "In whom ye also trusted, after that ye heard the word of truth, the gospel of your salvation: in whom also after that ye believed [upon believing], ye were sealed with that Holy Spirit of promise, Which is the earnest of our inheritance until the redemption of the purchased possession, unto the praise of his glory" (Eph. 1:13,14). We still have the complete inheritance coming, but the down payment which is the Holy Spirit has already been made.

It is no wonder then, that in the 5th chapter of Ephesians we are told not to be drunk with wine, but to be filled with the Holy Spirit (v. 18).

The sons of the prophets witnessed the power of God upon Elisha and they testified of the fact that the Spirit that energized Elijah rested upon their new leader.

The Spirit of God is likewise given to us, for the fulfilling of the appointed task entrusted to us. There is no excuse then, for us to say that we cannot do what God wants us to do. God does not ask us to do it, but to let the Holy Spirit do it in and through us. When we present our bodies and our all to Him, then He can work His purposes out in our lives.

Elijah's Office

Elisha was also the heir of the prophetic office. By this, we mean that he was to carry on the work that Elijah had begun. Elijah was a prophet and he had been God's man to rebuke the nation for its Baal worship and Elisha was to continue this ministry.

It is part of our heritage to carry on the work that our Saviour began. He had a physical body in which He was born, and lived, and died, and was buried. His body was resurrected and glorified, and in that body He is coming to earth again. But he has another Body and this is the Mystical Body of which you and I are members. He has left us here upon the earth to carry on the work. The Book of Acts opens with the words, "The former treatise have I made, O Theophilus, of all that Jesus began both to do and teach, Until the day in which he was taken up, after that he through the Holy Ghost had given commandments unto the apostles whom he had chosen." He made very clear to the disciples what their worldwide responsibility was.

How part of this was carried on is revealed in Acts 13 where we learn that as the early church ministered to the Lord, the Holy Spirit said, "Separate me Barnabas and Saul for the work whereunto I have called them" (Acts 13:2). According to Paul in II Corinthians 5:20, we are here to carry on the great ministry in the place of our Lord Jesus himself.

Perhaps no clearer words concerning this can be found anywhere than in John 20, beginning with verse 21, "Then said Jesus to them again, Peace be unto you: as my Father hath sent me, even so send I you. And when he had said this, he breathed on them, and saith unto them, Receive ye the Holy Ghost: Whose soever sins ye remit, they are remitted unto them; and whose soever sins ye retain, they are retained." This is a glorious heritage the Lord has left us! Let us accept it and act upon it.

CHAPTER FIFTEEN

LOOKING BACK AND LOOKING AHEAD

The reason for re-emphasizing some of the following aspects of Elijah's life is that we might not overlook any basic key to the understanding of the significance of his life to us.

A Man of Like Nature

In the first place, the Bible says he was a man subject to like passions, or as other translations have it, "a man of like nature" (James 5:17). God permits us to see where Elijah failed so that we need not think we are dealing with a man who was sent from heaven and was like us only in appearance, not in kind. He was altogether human like us; that which sets him apart from most of us is that he fully believed God.

The accomplishments possible to Elijah are just as possible to us today if God should call us to such a ministry and we will believe and trust Him for it. It is true that we know nothing of Elijah's family background or of his life before he burst suddenly on the scene of his public ministry. He came suddenly, and he went away suddenly. Yet he was a man who had the same fallen nature that we have; he was subject to temptations similar to ours, he faced the same tests and trials that human nature is subject to. He walked with the same God we have the privilege of walking with. He sought the Lord for the same things that you and I seek Him for. You and I may pray and seek the Lord as did Elijah, for our Saviour made very plain God's will in this matter: "Ask, and it shall be given you; seek, and ye shall find; knock, and it shall be opened unto you" (Matt. 7:7,8). The Apostle Paul said: "I can do all things through Christ which strengtheneth me" (Phil. 4:13).

Paul was no different than we are, save only that he was

193

called for a special task. He, too, like Elijah, gave himself wholeheartedly to the Lord to be used. God does not call us to be a Paul or an Elijah or an Elisha, but He calls on us to trust Him as they did and to be as fully given over to His will as they were. He has a task for us to do, and He equips us with all the necessary talents and abilities to do it. If we will present our bodies to Him He will work in us and through us. Remember, the Scripture says, "It is God which worketh in you both to will and to do of his good pleasure."

A Man of Faith

Another noteworthy factor in Elijah's life was that he walked by faith and not by sight. This makes all the difference in the world in the effectiveness of a life given over to the Lord. It was because he was a man of faith that he could live by the Brook Cherith even while it was drying up. The ravens brought him food in the morning and in the evening just as God said they would, and apparently it did not bother Elijah one bit that the water was slowly disappearing. It was an act of faith on his part that he went to live there in the first place, and he trusted God all the way through that experience. God had said what he was to do, and that settled it for Elijah (I Kings 17:2-7).

Later he went to live in the home of a widow woman who expected to cook her last morsel of bread and then she and her son would await death by starvation. But God multiplied the meal in the barrel and the oil in the cruse and all three lived in that home for several years. God provided day by day as the need arose. He did not give them large stores that would last for years, but His promise was that the daily supply would not cease, and it never did (I Kings 17:8-16).

Are we learning to trust God day by day? He never forgets or sleeps. He is always taking care of His own and is constantly looking for a child of His who will dare to believe Him. Elijah dared to consider God faithful who had promised. How often we have made God a liar by not believing Him! Nothing honors Him more than faith, but nothing so dishonors Him as unbelief.

When Elijah heard the word he believed it and acted upon it. Faith cometh by hearing and hearing by the Word of God.

Perhaps our faith is not larger than it is because we have not gone into the Word. Our faith will not grow if we do not take time to dwell in the Word of God itself.

I have talked to many people with spiritual problems, and when I have asked them concerning their personal devotional life I find it often very meager. They may read a little before they go to bed at night but they do not read the Bible in the morning because they are so busy. This ignoring of the Word is a basic reason for our problems.

It may not be always easy to take time in the morning for personal devotions, but if we would go on with the Lord and prosper under His hand we must take that time. We must get our sense of values properly adjusted and realize which is most important for our lives. The question is what do we consider more important—what we are doing, or what God wants to do in our lives. Starting out the day with God is the most important thing for any of us. This is what Elijah did, for He was a man of the Word who heard it and believed it and acted upon it.

Faith without works is dead and Elijah's faith was no dead faith. He acted on what he believed. Obedience is simply faith in action. Obedience trusts God and goes ahead.

A Man of Separation

In the third place, Elijah walked in complete separation from the evil around him. In many places people want Christian workers who are good mixers. They say this is necessary if we are going to win young people or some other group that are hard to reach or hard to hold. We feel they cannot be raised to our spiritual standard, so we get down to their low spiritual level. This is not the way God ordained reaching them, and it is not the way Elijah lived.

We are not called to win the world to Christ, but to witness against its sin with the Word of God. This is to be done by our outward life as well as by the Word. Elijah walked in manifest separation from the evil around him. He was a pilgrim and a stranger who never fraternized with evil in order to win evil men to the Lord's path.

He lived among such people, but he was not one with them in practice and belief. No doubt, many considered him unsocial and as having a "holier-than-thou" attitude. If we are right with God what difference will it make how we are charged by those who disagree with us? Let them go ahead and say what they want to say if our own lives before God are right and our hearts are humble. If we carry a "holier-than-thou" attitude then we are at fault. But just because someone accuses us of having such an attitude does not mean that we hold that attitude.

A Bible principle is laid down for us in Hebrews 13:13: "Let us go forth therefore unto him without the camp, bearing his reproach. For here have we no continuing city, but we seek one to come." Though this was not written in Elijah's day, nevertheless, this was the principle by which he lived. He was willing to suffer what was necessary in order to live where his Lord lived. His life was for the Lord and for Him alone.

This does not mean that we have to shut ourselves off from all contact and all responsibility to the society in which we live. We have to weigh our different responsibilities in the light of God's call to us for service. We need civic-minded Christians, but in such living they must by all means maintain a separated, holy life.

I am constantly under invitation to join this group and that group, but I realize if I were to do so it would be at the neglect of this work to which God has called me. To let lesser things interfere would be to disobey God.

A Man of Intercession

In the fourth place, Elijah was a man who was mighty in his intercession. This was not an easy task, but a hard one. His heart was constantly burdened for the people of Israel. His prayer on Mount Carmel is typical of the burden of his heart: "Lord God of Abraham, Isaac, and of Israel, let it be known this day that thou art God in Israel, and that I am thy servant, and that I have done all these things at thy word. Hear me, O Lord, hear me, that this people may know that thou art the Lord God, and that thou hast turned their heart back again"

(I Kings 18:36,37). Elijah was a great intercessor for his people. His prayers were largely on their behalf. This was one reason why God gave him such glorious vindication time after time.

In the fifth place, Elijah was a man of great courage. In order to understand this better we must distinguish clearly between natural bravery and spiritual boldness.

Elijah, when left to himself, was anything but brave. After he had dared to stand against Ahab and a hostile nation and the vindictive prophets of Baal, he fled when threatened by a woman (I Kings 18:21-19:3). As long as he dared to trust God he was as bold as a lion. The moment he took his eyes off God he was the opposite.

The man who truly fears God does not fear men.

God recorded all of this not to excuse us in our sin, but as a warning that when we do not stand with God even for a moment, we will fail and fall. Though greatly honored by God, Elijah's sins were not glossed over. Though he was endued with the power of the Holy Spirit in order to accomplish the tasks assigned to him, sin was never eradicated from his life. In his own flesh he was still a sinful man. This is why we are warned that we should take heed, because the person who thinks he stands can easily fall.

We are just as dependent upon God for the maintenance of our spiritual life and the spiritual graces He has given us as we are for God's bestowment of them upon us in the first place.

God vindicated the ministry of Elijah by taking him home without dying. Human nature being what it is, he was probably branded as an enthusiast, an alarmist, a firebrand, and his message brushed aside on these assumptions. Had he died a natural death some of these skeptics might have been confirmed in their unbelief. But when God took him away as He did, without dying, He placed His stamp of approval on the ministry of His prophet.

This is exactly what the Rapture will mean to the unbelieving church that presently pokes fun at the so-called fundamentalists, the people who believe their Bible. This event will be one of the most nerve-shaking events in all history, when millions of these "fanatical, Bible-believing Christians" will suddenly be gone and the apostate, ecumenical church left. That great event will vindicate those who have dared to believe the old-fashioned truth of the Word of God.

A sixth lesson we learn from Elijah's life is that it is not good for us to try to tell God how our lives should be lived. Elijah asked at one time that he might die, but God did not answer this plea, for He had something far better for His servant. God always has a better plan for us than we can ever devise, so let us never try to tell God what our lives should consist of.

Another thing we learn from Elijah's experience is that though he did not pass through death his translation helps us see what death is for the believer. It is not a state of being, but an act. It is not a condition, but a passage. There is no interval of unconsciousness. Real death is absence from the body for the believer, and being present with the Lord. By an act of birth we enter into natural life; by an act, which men call death, believers enter into and pass into real life.

The translation of the believer who will be on the earth when Christ returns for His Church is expressed very clearly in I Corinthians 15:51-53: "Behold, I shew you a mystery; We shall not all sleep, but we shall all be changed, In a moment, in the twinkling of an eye, at the last trump: for the trumpet shall sound, and the dead shall be raised incorruptible, and we shall be changed. For this corruptible must put on incorruption, and this mortal must put on immortality." This must be akin to the experience of Elijah when he was translated.

Elijah's Rewards

Some of Elijah's rewards are presented in Scripture. Others, we are sure, will not be in evidence until we all meet together in God's house.

This makes us consider some preliminary matters with regard to God's plans and the timing He ordains with regard to those plans. We are admonished in Galatians 6:9: "Let us not be weary in well doing: for in due season we shall reap, if we faint not." There is a great deal of mystery with regard to God's plan for any of us, but we must trust Him who has not called on us to understand what He does, but to trust Him for what He does. He has a long-range plan for this world into which each one of us has a part if we walk in obedience before the Lord.

In his letter James throws further light on this subject: "Be patient therefore, brethren, unto the coming of the Lord. Behold, the husbandman waiteth for the precious fruit of the earth, and hath long patience for it, until he receive the early and latter rain. Be ye also patient; stablish your hearts: for the coming of the Lord draweth nigh. Grudge not one against another, brethren, lest ye be condemned: behold, the judge standeth before the door" (James 5:7,8). This is again a reminder that we need patience with regard to the plans of God and constant trust in His wisdom, grace and power.

Still a third passage of Scripture that is very important with regard to this line of thought is the last part of the 11th chapter of Hebrews. This particular chapter lists great men and women of faith and concludes with this final word concerning them: "(Of whom the world was not worthy:) they wandered in deserts, and in mountains, and in dens and caves of the earth. And these all, having obtained a good report through faith, received not the promise: God having provided some better thing for us, that they without us should not be made perfect" (vv. 38-40). The Amplified translation of this section reads as follows: "[men] of whom the world was not worthy, roaming over the desolate places and the mountains, and [living] in caves and caverns and holes of the earth. And all of these, though they won divine approval by [means of] their faith, did not receive the fulfillment of what was promised. Because God had us in mind and had something better and greater in view for us, so that they [these heroes and heroines of faith] should not come to perfection apart from us, [that is, before we could join them]."

Your Part and Mine Are Vital

God has one great long-range plan and program with man that began with Adam and will conclude with the renovation of the heaven and the earth. Every part of this program will fit together and each believer will fill a place in it. We cannot see what is ahead nor do we know all that has been accomplished in the past. We do not even know what all is being done for the Lord in our own generation. But each one of us, as we walk with the Lord, fit into the plan that ties in with what has gone on in past generations and prepares the way for what is coming in future generations. This is why it is so essential for us to be obedient in every detail of our Christian experience. We may think our part is small and wonder how God could use us in His over all plan, but God overlooks nothing and to Him nothing is unimportant. It is for us to be sure that we fit in with the requirements that He lays down for us.

An illustration will help us here. In the plan of God Moses was God's great lawgiver. That was one of the great contributions he made during his service. Elijah, on the other hand, was God's great reformer to bring God's people back to the law of Moses. Each servant of the Lord, then, contributes his part to God's work and all will be included in the rewards given. The 11th chapter of Hebrews provides us with a small list of some who have had a part in God's work. This list is increased generation after generation, and you and I have a share in it.

Elijah on the Mount of Transfiguration

Elijah was not only chosen to witness in the days of Ahab, but on two occasions following that, hundreds of years apart. His earthly ministry was possibly for only 15 years, but he ministered again briefly on the Mount of Transfiguration and will come back to earth for another period to witness at a time still future.

When Elijah went to Horeb and heard the still small voice of God, he very possibly had little understanding of what God wanted from him. He had been discouraged because the revival he was looking for did not take place in his generation. It is very likely that when he appeared to the Lord Jesus on the

Mount of Transfiguration he understood in a better way what God's program involved.

This was a very important event in the life of our Lord and is recorded for us by three of the Gospel writers, Matthew in chapter 17, Mark in chapter 9 and Luke in chapter 9. Our Lord went to the top of a mountain to pray and took with him Peter, James and John. While He prayed we learn: "The fashion of his countenance was altered and His raiment was white and glistering. And, behold, there talked with him two men, which were Moses and Elias [Elijah]" (Luke 9:29,30).

This remarkable experience took place soon after the Lord had asked the disciples how people were identifying Him. Some thought He was John the Baptist, some thought He was Elijah, still others thought He was one of the other prophets.

Then it was that Peter spoke up and said, "Thou art the Christ, the Son of the living God" (Matt. 16:16). It was following this event that Jesus told His disciples about His death on the cross and His resurrection from the grave. Peter not understanding the meaning of Christ's words and what God's program was rebuked Him and said, "Be it far from thee, Lord: this shall not be unto thee" (Matt. 16:22).

This was one reason why Moses and Elijah were included in the transfiguration experience. They had played a significant part in Israel's history, Moses as the giver of the law and Elijah as the prophet who warned his people of the judgment that followed the breaking of the law. Now, they had come to meet the Saviour and talk with Him concerning a matter of even greater importance. They spoke to Him of His "decease which he should accomplish at Jerusalem" (Luke 9:31). The word "decease" is literally "exodus." They not only talked about His death, but about every part of the program of God that was ahead. The Calvary aspect of that hour was very near, and Moses and Elijah now could see what it all meant. Moses could now understand how the law was given to bring men to Christ. Elijah now understood why he preached judgment in his day, but did not see the completion of that program. Now he was about to see the grace of God manifested on behalf of all mankind. The suffering and dying of Jesus were the heart of it.

The Lord was to die and to be buried, but that was not all. It was His "exodus" they spoke of and that would include His rising from the grave and His departure to heaven.

These men had just come from heaven and they must have known how the hosts of heaven were electrified over what was about to take place on the earth. They spoke to our Saviour about it in the hearing of the disciples and this gave them a better understanding of God's program also. It was possibly also an encouragement for the Lord who was both God and man. He was facing death as a man which made this a serious hour for Him. So Moses and Elijah spoke to Him concerning the coming events. Elijah in particular, knowing something of the meaning of the still small voice, would talk about the grace of God which was now to be manifested.

Elijah's Final Witnessing

The Bible tells us that there is one further act in which Elijah will take part on the earth. The prophecy concerning this is in Malachi 4:5,6: "Behold, I will send you Elijah the prophet before the coming of the great and dreadful day of the Lord: And he shall turn the heart of the fathers to the children, and the heart of the children to their fathers, lest I come and smite the earth with a curse." This was foreshadowed in the coming of John the Baptist, but John made it very clear that he was not Elijah.

In Zechariah we learn that there will be two olive branches who will witness in a special way for the Lord in the latter days (4:2,3). Further details are given in the Book of the Revelation where we read: "And I will give power unto my two witnesses, and they shall prophesy a thousand two hundred and threescore days, clothed in sackcloth. These are the two olive trees, and the two candlesticks standing before the God of the earth. And if any man will hurt them, fire proceedeth out of their mouth, and devoureth their enemies: and if any man will hurt them, he must in this manner be killed." This is the very kind of thing that we saw in the experience of Elijah. Soldiers were sent to take him, but he prayed down fire from God which devoured them.

The time the passage of Revelation deals with is the second half of the seven-year Tribulation period. These witnesses have power to shut up heaven so that it does not rain and have power over the waters to turn them to blood and to smite the earth with plagues as often as they will. The withholding of the rain reminds us of Elijah and turning the water into blood and smiting the earth with plagues was done previously by Moses.

Though Moses is not spoken of in the Bible as coming back again in the sense that Elijah is spoken of, it seems reasonable to suppose that he is the second witness. He was on the Mount of Transfiguration with Elijah and the Saviour. We would not be dogmatic about this, for others identify the second witness as Enoch because as they point out, he did not die. Be that as it may, we know that one of them is Elijah. We further read concerning them: "And when they shall have finished their testimony, the beast that ascendeth out of the bottomless pit shall make war against them, and shall overcome them, and kill them. And their dead bodies shall lie in the street of the great city, which spiritually is called Sodom and Egypt, where also our Lord was crucified [old Jerusalem]. And they of the people and kindreds and tongues and nations shall see their dead bodies three days and an half, and shall not suffer their dead bodies to be put in the graves [will television be used to let the whole world see these men? Probably]. And they that dwell upon the earth shall rejoice over them, and make merry, and shall send gifts one to another; because these two prophets tormented them that dwelt on the earth. And after three days and an half the spirit of life from God entered into them, and they stood upon their feet; and great fear fell upon them which saw them. And they heard a great voice from heaven saying unto them, Come up hither. And they ascended up to heaven in a cloud; and their enemies beheld them" (vv. 8-12). This then is the picture. I call it the reward that God will give this man Elijah for his faithfulness.

We, too, shall be rewarded if we are faithful and true witnesses. If we are not ashamed of Him and suffer with Him, we shall rule and reign with Him.

CHAPTER SIXTEEN

ELIJAH'S GOD STILL LIVES

Assured of the fact that a double portion of Elijah's spirit rested on him, and knowing that the prophetic office was now his to carry on, Elisha demonstrated his faith when he came to the Jordan River and smote it with the mantle, asking this great question: "Where is the Lord God of Elijah?" (II Kings 2:14). This was not a question of doubt but a question that expected an affirmative answer. The Lord God of Elijah opened the waters for Elisha, just as He had done for Elijah.

This is still a question after 3000 years and is one that needs to be demonstrated in your life and mine. Too many people hold a very small view of God. They think of Him as Someone to run to when they are in trouble, but they call on Him only when they feel they need Him. Some are irreverent and border on the blasphemous as they think of our God, the Lord God of Elijah as the "man upstairs."

These low views of God lead to doctrinal errors. This is one reason why many people look to some kind of experience rather than to God himself. They want some gift of the Holy Spirit rather than the Holy Spirit himself. And low views of God contribute to a failure in applying Christian principles to conduct. Thousands of problems arise when we hold such views. We lack perfect obedience. We lack conviction of the sinfulness of sin because we do not see the holiness of God. We view Him more as we do ourselves than as the infinite God to be held in awe and respect.

How can we describe such a God when we ourselves are finite? We can tell you some things we have learned about Him or have experienced. Then, for some things in this closing section, I am indebted to the late A. W. Tozer who had a way of stating truth that is hard to improve on. His book *The Knowledge of the Holy* has been very helpful to me.

Elijah's God is the incomprehensible God; He is beyond human ability to fully understand or grasp. This is what Zophar meant when he said to Job, "Canst thou by searching find out God?" Our Lord said that no man knows the Father, save the Son. The Father can only be known through Jesus Christ our Lord. Furthermore, the things of God no man knows but the Spirit of God. Indeed, He is the incomprehensible God — but He is our God.

He is also the self-existent One. In the scientific realm every effect must have a cause. There can be no result without something having produced that result. There are scientists who honor God in their work, and there are others who want nothing to do with Him. They try to eliminate God from His universe because they cannot account for Him or explain Him.

Nevertheless, man is the recipient of life from God. It is a gift from God. Man is dependent upon Him. God is self-existent, but we must depend on Him for every breath we draw.

In his book Mr. Tozer illustrated this truth by reminding us about a sunbeam. When it is cut off from the sun it simply perishes. So man apart from God would pass out of the picture entirely if cut off from the benefits he receives from God. Elijah's God is the self-existent One and He is my God.

Elijah's God is the self-sufficient One. I can give nothing to Him that He has not first given to me. There is nothing above Him or beyond Him. He cannot be promoted, neither can He be degraded. Dr. Tozer wrote: "Were all human beings suddenly to become blind, still the sun would shine by day and the stars by night, for these owe nothing to the millions who benefit from their light. So, were every man on earth to become atheist, it could not affect God in any way. He is what He is in Himself without regard to any other. To believe in Him adds nothing to His perfections; to doubt Him takes nothing away."* He is the self-sufficient and self-existent God, and He is our God.

---

*The Knowledge of The Holy, Harper & Brothers, 1961.

God is not frustrated. He is never in need of our help and needs no defenders. He needs no one, yet when faith is present in a human heart He will work through any person whoever he be. Philippians 2:13 says, "He worketh in you both to will and to do of his good pleasure." But with all our work, even in faith, we can add nothing to God's self-sufficiency.

The God of Elijah is an eternal God. He dwells in all eternity. He has always existed. We are creatures of time and were created for eternity so that we could live with Him, but we had a beginning—God had none. Learn to know the God of Elijah. He is our God. Can you say for yourself: "He is my God"?

The God of Elijah is infinite. This means that everything that flows out of Him is infinite also. We are poor creatures, constantly frustrated, and hemmed in by all kinds of limitations from within and without. Is it not a wonderful and satisfying thing to turn to the God who is limitless in His powers and expressions? All nature has limitations, but God has none. His gift of eternal life is in Christ and it is limitless.

The believer has the life of God in him. This is the eternal life we receive through faith in Christ.

The mercy of God is infinite. His love is measureless and boundless. God as to His nature is love, and because He is infinite His love is infinite also. This is Elijah's God. This is our God.

Elijah's God is immutable or unchangeable. He never differs from Himself. He never varies from what He is. He never changes. He can never be more holy nor can He be less holy, for He is holiness itself. God has always been what He is and will always be what He has been. God does not change. He is the God of Abraham, and Abraham's unchanged God is my unchanged God.

Elijah's unchanged God is my unchanged God. There is wonderful comfort in knowing an unchanging God in a changing world. "I am the Lord, I change not," says Malachi about his God. With all our scientific knowledge we have not changed God. The sad fact is that our scientific knowledge has not brought us any closer to knowing God. Only through the Word can He be known, and He is unchanging.

Elijah's God is omniscient, that is, He is all-knowing. Psalm 139 is a classic portion of Scripture dealing with this subject. It is a Psalm that can frighten us if we are running from God, but it can comfort if we are being tested and afflicted. God knows all about us. And His knowledge about us is perfect knowledge. His knowledge has never been less so that He had to learn more. He does not need to learn anything and He has not learned anything, for His perfection of knowledge cannot be added to. In Isaiah 40:13,14 is this statement: "Who hath directed the Spirit of the Lord, or being his counsellor hath taught him? With whom took he counsel, and who instructed him, and taught him in the path of judgment, and taught him knowledge, and shewed to him the way of understanding?"

God knows all things. If knowledge could be added to Him, He would be imperfect and therefore could not be God. God never discovers anything, for He knows all things. He is never surprised and amazed, for nothing ever catches Him unawares. He knows us through and through. He is all-wise. In fact, it says concerning Christ, that He has been made unto us "wisdom." Elijah's wise God is our God.

Elijah's God is also known as the omnipotent God; that is, the Almighty One. He is all-powerful and sovereign. He has the right to do as He wants, and He has the power to do what He wants. In order to reign God must have power. As sovereign, what He wants to do He can do any time, for He has the right to do so. But in order to do so, He must be the all-powerful God. This is Elijah's God, and my God. Do you recognize Him as yours?

While God has delegated certain power to His creatures, He has not lost any power in doing so. He is still the same God. Science discovers how God's power operates, but science does not add to God's power. We do not know what electricity is, but we are learning how to use it. We do not know all there is to know about atomic power, but we are slowly learning how to put it to good use. But these are powers in what we call nature; but God, our God and Elijah's God, the all-powerful One, is the God of nature.

Elijah's God is omnipresent. This simply means that God is everywhere present at the same time. He is close to everything and next to everyone. God is above, and beneath, and beside all things. He fills within, and He surrounds without, and cannot be excluded from anything. But this does not mean that God and His universe are one and the same. He is separate and apart from what He has created, and yet He is present with it at all times.

The climax of all of this is that Elijah's God is a faithful God. He cannot deny Himself. A failure to be faithful would mean imperfection. God is perfect, so that unfaithfulness could not occur in Him. We can count on Him to be faithful in everything He has promised to do for us. Since God is who He is, He cannot be different than what He is. He must remain faithful in all His words and acts.

But He is beyond all of this, for if we could describe God in human language then God would be no more than another human being. So He is all we have said and much more.

"O the depth of the riches both of the wisdom and knowledge of God! how unsearchable are his judgments, and his ways past finding out! For who hath known the mind of the Lord? or who hath been his counsellor? Or who hath first given to him, and it shall be recompensed unto him again? For of him, and through him, and to him, are all things: to whom be glory for ever. Amen" (Rom. 11:33-36).

Elijah's God Still Lives

Elijah made a sacrifice
To offer to Jehovah;
It had been wet with water thrice,
Baal's sacrifice was over;
Elijah pray'd, the fire came down,
And lick'd the water all around,
And doubting ones believ'd and found
Elijah's God was living.

Elijah's God still lives today,
And answers still by fire;

My friend, just let Him have His way,
He'll grant your heart's desire,
Consume the sacrifice you make
And bid your slumb'ring soul awake,
And chains of inbred sin will break,
Elijah's God is living.

Elijah's God still lives today,
To take the guilt of sin away;
And when I pray my heart's desire,
Upon my soul He sends down fire.
                              —Rev. W. Grum

You have a mirror-

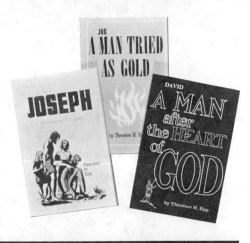

the kind that shows how you look outside. Perhaps you need another mirror—the kind that shows how you look inside.

The Bible is full of such mirrors, but foremost among them are the Bible characters. Look deeply into their lives and see yourself reflected. Find victory in your life as you see how they became victorious. Escape sorrow and tragedy as you avoid the mistakes they made.

These books by Theodore H. Epp can be a tremendous encouragement to the believer today. For if God could do such a work then, He can also work in believers' lives today.

DAVID, A MAN AFTER THE HEART OF GOD
215 pages.
$1.50 each   1295-4

JOB, A MAN TRIED AS GOLD
222 pages.
$2.00 each   1293-8

JOSEPH: 'GOD PLANNED IT FOR GOOD'
143 pages.
$1.50 each   1283-0

BACK TO THE BIBLE BROADCAST
Box 82808, Lincoln, Nebraska 68501 or
Box 10, Winnipeg, Manitoba R3C 2G2